RANDY CHARLES EPPING

A BEGINNER'S GUIDE

TO THE WORLD ECONOMY

Randy Charles Epping, an American citizen based in
Zurich, Switzerland, has worked in international
finance for many years, holding management positions in European and American investment banks in
London, Geneva, and Zurich. He has a master's
degree in International Relations from Yale University in addition to degrees from the University of
Paris-Sorbonne and the University of Notre Dame.
He is currently the manager of IFS Project Management AG, a Switzerland-based international consulting company. He is also the president of the Central
Europe Foundation. Mr. Epping is fluent in six languages: English, French, German, Italian, Portuguese,
and Spanish.

A BEGINNER'S GUIDE TO THE

WORLD ECONOMY

A BEGINNER'S GUIDE TO THE
WORLD
ECONOMY

*Eighty-one Basic Economic Concepts
That Will Change the Way
You See the World*

RANDY CHARLES EPPING

VINTAGE BOOKS
A DIVISION OF RANDOM HOUSE, INC.
NEW YORK

THIRD VINTAGE BOOKS EDITION, APRIL 2001

Copright © 1992, 1995, 2001 by Randy Charles Epping
Maps copyright © 2001 by Robert Bull

Maps on pages xx and xxi by Robert Bull, based on two maps "National Income" and "Population" from *The State of the World Atlas, 6th Edition,* by Dan Smith (Penguin, London and New York). Copyright © MyriadEditions.com. Reproduced with permission of Myriad Editions Limited, Brighton, England.

Library of Congress Cataloging-in-Publication Data
Epping, Randy Charles.
A beginner's guide to the world economy : eighty-one basic economic concepts that will change the way you see the world / Randy Charles Epping.
p. cm.
ISBN 0-375-72579-2 (pbk.)
1. International finance. 2. Finance. I. Title: World economy. II. Title.
HG3881 .E573 2001
332'. 042—dc21   00-050968

Book design by Robert Bull Design

www.vintagebooks.com

Printed in the United States of America
10 9 8

If economists want to be understood, let them use plainer words . . . [and] address those words less to politicians and more to everybody else. Politicians care about what voters think, especially voters in blocks, and not a shred about what economists think. Talking to politicians about economics is therefore a waste of time. The only way to make governments behave as if they were economically literate is to confront them with electorates that are.

—*The Economist*

This book is dedicated to Jerrod, Rick, and Mark—to whom the future really does belong.

I would like to thank everyone who helped me make this book as user-friendly as possible: Jim Ragsdale in Paris; Shawn and Charlie Engelberg in Lake Oswego, Oregon; Rick Fuller in Portland; Alex Neumann in Zurich; Sebastian Velasco in Madrid; Emanuele Pignatelli and Benoit Demeulemeester in Zurich; Janos Faragó and Rich Rimer in Geneva; Sigbert Feller in Auserberg, Switzerland; Rodrigo Fiães in Rio de Janeiro; Pedro, Marisa, and João Moreira Salles in São Paulo; Anders Thomsen in Copenhagen; Enrique Schmid in San Pedro Sula, Honduras; Mohamed Ben Ali in Hammam-Sousse, Tunisia; Chung Mak in Hong Kong; Robert Malley in Washington, D.C.; Jim Crystal in Portland; Jean-Marc and Virginia Pilpoul in Paris; Del Franz in New Hope, Pennsylvania; Joanna Hurley in Albuquerque; Persio Arida in São Paulo; and Michael Piore at MIT in Cambridge, Massachusetts.

I would also like to thank my editors at Vintage Books: Marty Asher, for his vision and confidence in developing this book as a Vintage Original, and Edward Kastenmeier for his tireless efforts in the preparation of this new edition. Many thanks to Megan Hustad as well.

Finally, I would like to thank the readers who have contacted me with comments and suggestions over the years. This book is for you.

CONTENTS

INTRODUCTION

WHAT'S THE WORLD coming to? In Seattle, people are tear-gassed and thrown in jail for protesting the World Trade Organization. In France, a woman is killed when "anti-globalization" terrorists blow up a local McDonald's. Companies around the world are being boycotted for not paying enough to their Third World employees. And economic summits from Washington to Prague to Davos to Melbourne have been disrupted by rabidly anti-global crowds.

An interesting insight into what is driving this anti-globalization movement could be found in Portland, Oregon, recently where voter-led tax cuts forced local schools to close down extracurricular activities, including some high-school sports programs. A local sports-shoe manufacturer with global operations stepped in with a multimillion dollar donation to help the schools out. The students were elated, but one of the school board members refused to accept the money because it came from a company that was "exploiting" workers in poor countries. I happened to be in Portland at the time, and was approached by a group of concerned citizens who asked me to sign a petition to help out the cash-strapped schools by increasing taxes on—you guessed it—local corporations. "We're not going to tax people," they reassured me, "we're going to tax businesses—especially the ones that earn their money immorally by paying foreign workers only a dollar an hour."

Fuzzy economic thinking is sometimes excusable, but when it leads to unforeseen consequences for the poor on the other side of the world, it can be disastrous. Imagine you and your family are living in the squalor of an overcrowded Third World city and one day you get a job in a relatively well-paying foreign-owned factory—but then your boss comes to you and says they are going to close the factory because of the difficulty of convincing rich-country protesters that a dollar an hour is, in fact, a lot of money in a country where an entire family can live on a few dollars a day.

Obviously, every participant in the world economy has the responsibility to see that workers and children are not exploited and that no one is forced to work at a job that is inappropriate. And everyone needs to verify that companies around the world are respecting the environment and providing basic workers' rights. But to say that paying a dollar an hour is "immoral" without understanding the economic background is reckless—at best. Is it immoral for a schoolteacher in South Dakota to be paid $29,000 when a schoolteacher in Connecticut is paid $52,000?

Globalization . . . income gaps between rich and poor . . . trade wars . . . the New Economy. A virtual explosion of complexity has taken place in the world economy over the last few years, and we are being asked to understand it all. Words and phrases like "hedge funds," "WTO," "stock options," and "economic sanctions" appear regularly in the news, and many of us are at a loss.

But if we are going to succeed in this new world economy, we have to be able to understand at least the basics. Whoever we are—environmentalists or farmers, college students or business people, homemakers or union activists—if we're going to be responsible citizens and consumers, we're going to have to become economically literate.

For many of us, however, the study of economics has been an exercise in futility, full of obscure graphs and equations—and hopelessly out of touch with our daily lives. This doesn't have to

be the case. In fact, the world economy is really no more complicated than the domestic economy we experience every day. We
don't think twice about crossing the street to deposit our money
in a bank that provides a better interest rate than the one next
door. In an expanding global economy, we shouldn't think twice
about crossing borders to invest our money or sell our goods and
services.

The Internet and the rapidly expanding possibilities for
cross-border communication are allowing the world economy to
touch our lives in ways unheard of just a few years ago—from
new jobs, goods, and services to new threats to our economic
welfare. By understanding the basics about the world economy,
we will be able to make better decisions about where we want
this world to go. And with economically literate voters pushing
them on, politicians will start making more rational economic
decisions as well—leading to a more prosperous and maybe even
a more socially conscious and environmentally sound world in
the years to come.

In this new edition of *A Beginner's Guide*, I have incorporated numerous readers' comments. (Please feel free to e-mail me
anytime at: RCEpping@aya.yale.edu.) Many readers from around
the world have cited this book as instrumental in helping them
take their first steps in the global economy—Third World aid
workers, e-commerce professionals, students, and executives.
Whoever we are and wherever we live, we need to understand the
basics if we are going to get involved in the world economy. And
sooner or later, we all get involved—one way or another.

Remember, this is not meant to be a "get-rich-quick" book;
it won't tell you which foreign dot-coms to invest in or how to
corner the international currency markets. But any successful
foray into the global marketplace must be accompanied by a
thorough understanding of the principles on which the global

markets are based. Imagine trying to invest in an e-commerce IPO without first knowing your way around the Internet.

I hope you enjoy this book. It was fun to write and should be fun to read. I have used no graphs and no equations, and statistics are always accompanied by examples to give meaning to the numbers.

A Beginner's Guide to the World Economy, as the name implies, will cover only the basic concepts that you are exposed to in your daily life. Complicated economic theories and principles will be left to others.

How to begin? Although it may be useful to start with the general economic concepts found at the beginning of the book, each section can be read individually. The book can be read from front to back, from back to front, or sections can be read at random—whatever works best for you. The glossary at the end can also be used for quick reference in the future when unfamiliar terms reappear in the news, on the Web, or in daily conversation.

The world economy can be easily understood. Once we understand the basics, the global economy can become a great adventure, where foreign lands and peoples interact in fascinating ways. It just has to be simply explained. Enjoy!

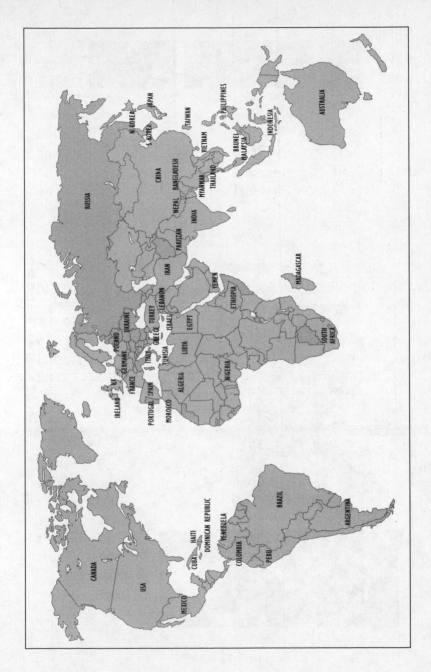

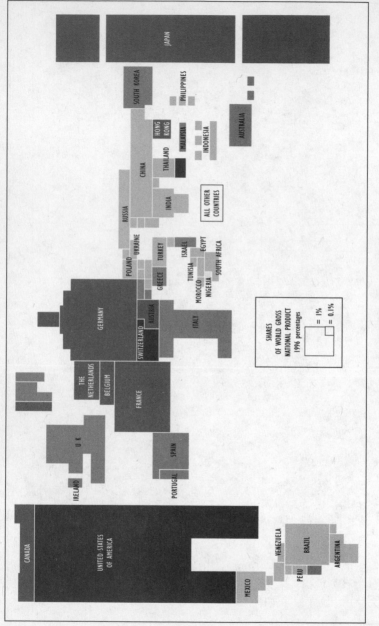

CANADA

UNITED STATES
OF AMERICA

IRELAND

U K

PORTUGAL

SPAIN

THE NETHERLANDS

BELGIUM

FRANCE

SWITZERLAND

GERMANY

AUSTRIA

ITALY

POLAND

GREECE

UKRAINE

TURKEY

RUSSIA

ISRAEL

TUNISIA

MOROCCO

NIGERIA

EGYPT

SOUTH AFRICA

INDIA

CHINA

SOUTH KOREA

PHILIPPINES

HONG KONG

THAILAND

MALAYSIA

INDONESIA

AUSTRALIA

JAPAN

MEXICO

VENEZUELA

PERU

BRAZIL

ARGENTINA

ALL OTHER
COUNTRIES

SHARES
OF WORLD GROSS
NATIONAL PRODUCT
1996 percentages

☐ = 1%

▫ = 0.1%

NATIONAL INCOME

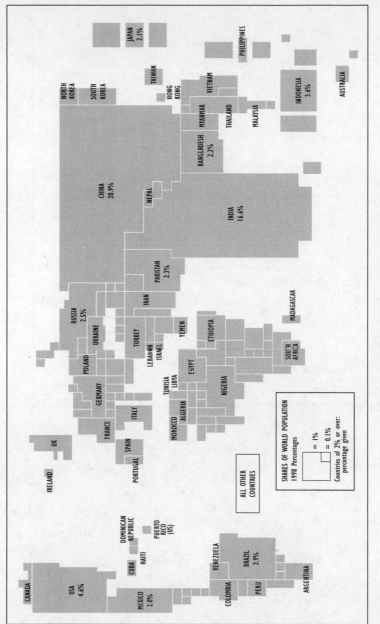

POPULATION

A BEGINNER'S GUIDE TO THE

WORLD
ECONOMY

1. WHAT IS THE WORLD ECONOMY?

IN MANY WAYS, we are all part of the world economy. When we drink our imported morning coffee, when we download music from a foreign Web site, or when we travel abroad on vacation, we are all participating in the growing world of international trade and finance.

And it is not only as a consumer of imported goods and services that we are part of the world economy. The money that our pension funds or college endowments invest in foreign markets will help pay for our retirements or for a new dormitory on campus. Foreign investors in our home economies also provide needed jobs for our friends and families. Even a local athlete who has signed a contract to play abroad is considered an export in economic terms.

The world economy consists of all those interactions among people, businesses, and governments that cross international borders—even the illegal ones. If we buy drugs—or if we join the fight against drugs by helping Latin American farmers substitute food crops for coca—we are participating in the world of international trade. Even a boycott of goods and services, such as those that endanger certain species of animals or those that come from countries that abuse human rights, make us part of the world economy.

Being part of the world economy is no longer just buying a foreign-made television or traveling to Mexico on spring break; it's also using the Internet to do business abroad or making sure that our individual retirement funds are invested in socially responsible companies around the world. Basically, anything that crosses an international border—any good, service, or transfer of funds—makes us part of the expanding world of international trade and finance.

2. HOW IS WEALTH DETERMINED AROUND THE WORLD?

A NATION'S WEALTH CAN best be determined by looking at its people. But what aspects do we look at first? Are Japanese workers better off because they have higher salaries than Canadians? Are Swedish consumers better off because they have more mobile telephones than Brazilians? Are the Italians better off because they have a higher savings rate than Americans?

There are many different ways to determine wealth. Most economists define wealth as what a person owns, such as stocks, real estate, and money in the bank. However, most people look first to their income to see how well off they are. The problem in comparing incomes around the world is that most countries use different currencies. Is a French salary of 100,000 euros worth more than an English salary of 80,000 British pounds? Not if a pound is worth almost two euros.

Also, exchange rates are constantly fluctuating, and the "price" of each currency is determined by foreign exchange markets around the world just as the value of wheat or apples is determined—by the law of supply and demand. No one really knows what a currency is worth (see *What Are Freely Floating Currencies?*). Basically a currency is simply worth whatever someone is willing to pay for it. For example, if the foreign exchange markets think that the Mexican economy is set to boom, they'll buy Mexican pesos and sell euros or yen or any other currencies they think will be relatively weak in the years to come.

Comparing wealth around the world is also made difficult by differences in the *cost of living* from one country to another. If a Big Mac or a two-room apartment costs twice as much in Tokyo as in Los Angeles, a high salary in Japan doesn't necessarily mean that a Japanese worker is better off. A salary is only worth what it can buy—and that depends on the local prices of goods and services.

Economists have, therefore, set up a system to adjust each country's currency by its "purchasing power." This is done by looking at the goods and services that people usually purchase in their daily lives. The price of this "basket" of products—including everything from housing to haircuts, from food to movie tickets—is then compared between countries, giving us a more reliable exchange rate, usually referred to as *purchasing power parity (PPP)*.

Most PPP's, however, are based on a basket of goods and services used by people in rich countries, which skews the results somewhat. The monthly purchases of a primary school teacher in Paris are obviously quite different from those of a teacher in Jakarta, who could rarely afford such "luxuries" as high-tech medical care or air travel. For example, if the spending patterns of teachers in developing countries were used to determine the PPP in the following list, the PPP adjusted salaries in India, Kenya, or Indonesia would be significantly higher.

In an attempt to make things simple, *The Economist* has resorted to calculating a PPP using the price of hamburgers around the world, called the Big Mac Index. This still doesn't solve the problem, however—even a McDonald's hamburger is considered a luxury in some countries. In Nairobi, for example, it takes an average worker almost three hours to earn enough to buy a Big Mac; in Los Angeles or Tokyo, it takes about ten minutes.

However calculated, purchasing power parity does provide us with valuable insights into what salaries actually buy in each country, giving us a better idea of who in the world is really better off.

AVERAGE SALARIES AROUND THE WORLD

(Primary School Teacher)

	NOMINAL SALARY (USING US$ EXCHANGE RATE)	REAL SALARY (ADJUSTED FOR PURCHASING POWER)
Japan (Tokyo)	$47,900	$30,486
United States (Los Angeles)	$43,100	$43,100
Germany (Frankfurt)	$36,600	$42,783
Great Britain (London)	$35,800	$33,644
Canada (Toronto)	$34,700	$41,285
Australia (Sydney)	$27,300	$34,347
France (Paris)	$20,100	$21,956
Italy (Milan)	$18,500	$24,672
Spain (Madrid)	$18,400	$29,533
Israel (Tel Aviv)	$14,100	$15,541
Argentina (Buenos Aires)	$5,200	$6,049
Mexico (Mexico City)	$4,900	$7,020
Brazil (São Paulo)	$4,300	$6,470
China (Shanghai)	$2,900	$2,994
Hungary (Budapest)	$2,400	$4,694
India (Mumbai)	$1,700	$4,055
Kenya (Nairobi)	$1,200	$1,969
Indonesia (Jakarta)	$900	$1,537

Source: Prices and Earnings Around the Globe—2000 Edition, UBS Switzerland.

3. WHAT IS MACROECONOMICS?

MACROECONOMICS PROVIDES US with a bird's-eye view of a country's economic landscape. Instead of looking at the behavior of individual businesses and consumers—referred to as *microeconomics*—the goal of macroeconomics is to look at overall economic trends such as employment levels, productivity, and inflation. The study of the world economy is, therefore, essentially a *macroeconomic* survey.

Basically, a country's economy is controlled by its money supply—just as the speed of an engine is regulated by its fuel supply—and each country's *monetary policy* is the responsibility of its central bank. The Bank of England, the European Central Bank, and the Bank of Japan all regulate their money supply with the same basic goals as the U.S. Federal Reserve: to promote economic growth while keeping inflation in check. Just as the driver uses an accelerator to speed up or slow down a vehicle, central banks control the economy by increasing or decreasing the money supply (see *What Is a Central Bank?*).

Monetary policy is a guessing game of sorts. Despite the tendency of the news media to concentrate on the latest economic statistics, there is no one single indicator that tells us how fast an economy is growing—or if that growth will lead to inflation. Also there is no way to know how quickly an economy will respond to political or fiscal changes that may take months or years to implement. Consumers usually do not rush out to buy new houses as soon as a central bank announces lower interest rates.

Central banks, therefore, need to be prescient, keeping one

eye on inflation, which is the product of an overheating economy, and one eye on unemployment, which is the product of a slowing economy. The booming U.S. economy in the 1990s was a perfect example of how economic growth could reduce unemployment levels to the point where it is necessary to slow down the economy or face a resurgence of inflation (see *What Is the New Economy?*).

Government spending, taxation, and borrowing—called *fiscal policy*—also affects the economy, although not as drastically as monetary policy. However, just as a family's economic health is influenced by the parents' earning and spending habits, a nation's economic health is heavily influenced by fiscal policy. For better or for worse, the major economic influences on our daily lives are essentially the result of macroeconomic decisions.

4. HOW DOES INTERNATIONAL TRADE WORK?

WHEN THE SWISS export chocolate to Honduras, they can use the money they earn to import Honduran bananas—or they can use it to pay for Kuwaiti oil or vacations in Hawaii. The basic idea of international trade and investment is simple: each country produces goods or services that can either be consumed at home or exported abroad. The money earned from these exports can then be used to pay for imports of other goods and services.

The main difference between domestic and international trade is the use of foreign currencies, and goods crossing international borders can be paid for in any internationally accepted currency. It is all the same, as long as the money ends up in the pocket of the exporter.

Most trade is added up in U.S. dollars, although the trading itself often involves a myriad of currencies. In Montreal, someone importing Japanese CD players first pays Sony Japan in yen. Then, when the CD player is sold at a record store on the *rue de l'Université*, the importer is paid in Canadian dollars—which are then exchanged for yen to pay for more imports.

Trade and investment is a two-way street: what goes out as exports of goods and services comes back in—in the form of money. And money flowing into an economy doesn't just sit around collecting dust. It is usually invested, or it is used to purchase goods and services—both at home and abroad. When a hardworking country exports more than it imports, it ends up with money to invest in the global economy.

It is hard to convince anti-globalization protesters that trade ends up making both sides better off, but it does. One only need look at rich countries around the world down through history. Those nations that opened their borders to trade were the ones who prospered: ancient Greece, medieval China, renaissance Italy, golden-age Holland, nineteenth-century England, postwar America, and now, almost every country in the world economy.

Great wealth comes from trading, and there is a reason. No country would sell something abroad unless it could make a profit somehow. This profit then is used to make life better for the economy as a whole. Even if the money is not distributed evenly—which is a social issue that every country has to deal with—it does not mean that people are worse off because of trade. With a minimum of trade barriers, consumers are given the opportunity to buy the best products at the best prices. By opening up markets, a government allows its citizens to export those things that they are best at producing and to import the rest, choosing from the best the world has to offer.

By opening up borders to trade, rich countries are also able to stimulate growth in the developing countries—which often makes both sides better off. By importing cheaper goods from the developing countries, the industrialized countries not only provide their own consumers with a wider range of products to choose from, they stimulate the growth of jobs in countries where people are desperate to earn enough to live on. By giving the developing countries an economic "jump start," rich countries are able to expand their own economies as well.

As developing countries grow and their citizens suddenly have disposable income, the first things they usually buy are goods and services from the industrialized countries, such as automobiles, movies, and computers. In the end, increased trade leads to more growth, which means more jobs for almost everyone (see *What Causes the Income Gap Between Rich and Poor Countries?*).

When a country decides to erect trade barriers, the result usually damages everyone—including those people the barriers were originally meant to protect. The Great Depression of the 1930s, for example, spread around the world when the United States decided to erect trade barriers to protect local producers. As other countries retaliated, trade plummeted, jobs were lost, and the world entered a long period of economic decline.

5. WHAT IS GLOBALIZATION?

THE AMERICAN ACTRESS Joan Crawford once said, "The only thing worse than being talked about is not being talked about." Countries that have seen their borders opened by the forces of global trade and finance could say something similar: the only thing worse than opening your economy to the world is *not* opening it.

Many critics of globalization say that it is a major cause of poverty, that it opens up developing countries to exploitation by big foreign corporations, and that it results in people in wealthy countries losing jobs when cheaper foreign imports put their companies out of business. They also criticize foreigners for "buying up" local companies and creating a homogenized world run by multinational corporations not accountable to any government.

Capitalism, it must be said, is by no means a perfect system. People do lose jobs, and some people do earn a lot more money than others. In centrally planned socialist economies, jobs and income are guaranteed at fixed levels for life; in a capitalist economy nothing is guaranteed, especially not equality of income. But it also must be said that, despite all its faults, capitalism is the best system we have for eliminating poverty and creating wealth. One need only look at the crumbling economies of Eastern Europe to see that socialism, despite its claim to distribute the wealth evenly, ends up essentially with little wealth to distribute to anyone.

Globalization, for all its faults, helps economies grow— which means improving standards of living for billions of people around the world. The UN Human Development Index, an indicator of literacy, longevity, and standard of living in countries around the world, shows that during the last years of the twentieth century, more than a billion people around the world escaped absolute poverty through economic growth. Those countries that embraced globalization, especially those in the Third World, have enjoyed rates of growth that were, on average, 50 percent higher than those with closed borders.

For many people in developing countries, economic growth is the ultimate antipoverty weapon. It means access to clean water, a safe house to live in, and a chance to educate their children to prepare for a better future. Countries with expanding economies also enjoy greater political freedom, more social spending, and higher standards of living, for both rich and poor (see *What Causes the Income Gap Between Rich and Poor Countries?*).

Even in the United States, the economic boom of the 1990s was fueled in no small part by globalization. Open borders allowed new ideas and technology to flow in freely from around the globe, fueling an increase in productivity. Living standards went up when consumers and businesses were able to buy from countries that had a *comparative advantage,* producing better-made products at better prices. Free trade has also kept local producers on their toes, making them more efficient and forcing them to keep their own prices in line with those from other countries. In addition, export-oriented jobs generally pay more than those that are dependent on the local economy.

Globalization, it must be noted, does benefit some people more than others. Access to technology and capital has created many new jobs for workers in developing countries, and those countries and companies with technology and capital to sell have also benefited enormously from globalization. For example, millions of information technology jobs have been created in Ireland and India—not just in Silicon Valley.

Those left out, especially the high-salary workers in developed countries with little or no education, have seen millions of jobs taken away by newly productive Third World workers, and until they get the training and education they need to find new jobs, they will justifiably blame the world economy for their loss.

6. WHAT ARE TRADE SURPLUSES AND DEFICITS?

LIKE ANY BUSINESS, a country has to keep track of its inflow and outflow of goods, services, and payments. At the end of any given period, every country has to look at its "bottom line" and add up all international trade and investment. During the 1990s, for example, the United States was one of the world's most profligate economies, running yearly trade deficits of hundreds of billions of dollars.

The narrowest measure of a country's trade, the *merchandise trade balance,* counts only "visible" goods such as motorcycles, wine, and laptops. This measure is often referred to in the press as the "trade balance" even though it actually includes only *tangible* goods—those that can be loaded on a ship, an airplane, or any other means of transport that moves goods from one country to another.

In today's high-tech world, it is much more important to look at total trade—including services such as tourism and movies. When services are added into the picture, a country's trade balance is called a *current account.* It may not be obvious, but many countries' exports and imports of services constitute a big part of their foreign trade. Hollywood movies, for example, consistently earn more money abroad than they do in the United States. Tourism, for many countries, such as Italy or Mexico, also provides enormous earnings. A tourist's purchase of hotel and restaurant services abroad counts for just as much as a consumer at home buying an imported microwave.

The current account shows us which countries have been profitable traders—running a trade surplus, with money in the bank at the end of the year—and which countries have been profligate, spending more abroad than they have earned. This information has a huge affect on a country's currency. Countries with a current account *surplus* often use their extra money to invest abroad—or simply put the money in their national "cookie jar" of *foreign currency reserves,* which are usually held at the central bank.

In theory, no country can run a current account deficit indefinitely. Before long, a country running a consistent trade deficit will see its currency decline in value as it buys more and more foreign money to pay for imports. The United States was able to buck this trend for much of the 1990s as foreign money poured in, mostly in the form of investment in the booming U.S. economy.

Countries running a current account deficit usually look abroad for financing, either in the form of loans or investments from abroad. Since most countries are loathe to see their assets being bought up by foreigners, they try to run trade surpluses or dip into their foreign exchange reserves to pay the difference. All these payments in and out constitute the country's *capital account.*

The widest measure of a country's trade is called the *balance of payments.* It includes not only goods and services, but also all the payments from the country's capital account. It is called a "balance" because, in theory, all the payments in and out add up at the end of the year. Every banana, every automobile, every investment—basically every payment that crosses a country's borders—is included in this final tally of international trade and investment.

7. WHAT IS MONEY?

CONTRARY TO POPULAR belief, money does not make the world go round—the global economy runs on the trade of goods and services. But without money, trade would be a very difficult undertaking indeed. Imagine sending strawberries to France and waiting to be paid with the next shipment of cheese. Or imagine wanting to keep some of your earnings as a nest egg—Roquefort wouldn't keep very well in a bank. And how many strawberries is a piece of cheese worth, anyway?

These issues can all be resolved by using something that represents value. It's called money. Whether it's a piece of paper or a chunk of metal or a credit at your online bank, money serves three purposes: it serves as a *medium of exchange,* allowing you to sell your strawberries for something more convenient than cheese; it allows people to *store value* from one year to the next—money doesn't spoil like cheese; and it serves as a *unit of account,* telling us how much things are worth by providing us with a point of reference that is universally understood.

The earliest money, shells and beads, served the same role that paper, credit cards, and electronic transfers serve today: money makes trade manageable. By serving as a medium of exchange, money acts as a go-between. When you sell something for money, you can use it to buy other products.

In addition, by using money to store value, you make it possible to look beyond the horizons of a few days or weeks. As opposed to perishable commodities, money will always be around. After selling goods or services for money, the seller can sit back and wait for the best time to purchase other goods and services. During this time, money can be stuffed under a mattress or it can be invested. If it is invested wisely, it can keep pace with inflation—or even outpace it.

Finally, by using money as a unit of account, goods and services from around the world can be evaluated by using a common unit of measure. Money not only tells us how many strawberries a piece of cheese is worth, it tells us how many hours of your work it takes to buy an airplane ticket, or how many hamburgers it would take to buy a car. By allowing for all goods and services to be expressed in terms of a standardized unit, worldwide trade is made immeasurably easier.

MAJOR CURRENCIES AROUND THE WORLD AND THEIR EXCHANGE RATES

COUNTRY	CURRENCY	VALUE (IN UNITS PER U.S. DOLLAR)			
		1985	1990	1995	2000
Asia/Pacific					
Australia	dollar	1.5	1.3	1.3	1.8
China	yuan	2.8	4.7	8.4	8.3
Hong Kong	dollar	7.8	7.8	7.7	7.8
India	rupee	12.1	17.8	31.4	46.7
Japan	yen (¥)	201	136	100	113
Malaysia	ringgit	2.5	2.7	2.5	3.8
New Zealand	dollar	2.0	1.7	1.6	2.3
Africa					
Kenya	shilling	14.7	24.0	44.9	78.6
Morocco	dirham	9.6	8.0	8.9	10.6

Senegal, Gabon	CFA franc	378	254	534	706
South Africa	rand	2.6	3.4	3.5	7.5

The Americas

Argentina	peso	0.8*	5.58	1.0*	1.0
Brazil	real	10,400	170*	0.8*	1.9
Canada	dollar	1.4	1.2	1.4	1.5
Chile	peso	232	298	395	574
Mexico	peso	457	2,941		5.1*	9.5

Europe

**Austria	schilling (euro)	17.3	10.5	10.9	14.8
**Belgium	franc (euro)	50.4	31.0	31.8	43.4
Britain	pound (£)	0.7	0.5	0.6	0.7
Denmark	krone	9.0	5.8	6.1	8.1
**Euro area countries	euro (€)	—	—	—	0.9
**Finland	markka (euro)	5.4	3.6	4.7	6.4
**France	franc (euro)	7.6	5.1	5.4	7.1
**Germany	mark (euro)	2.5	1.5	1.6	2.1
**Greece	drachma (euro)	148	156	241	367
**Italy	lira (euro)	1,683	1,128	1,621	2,084
**Netherlands	guilder (euro)	2.8	1.7	1.7	2.4
Norway	krone	7.6	5.9	6.8	8.8
**Portugal	escudo (euro)	159	132	160	216
**Spain	peseta (euro)	154	95	132	179
Sweden	krona	7.6	5.6	7.4	9.5
Switzerland	franc	2.1	1.3	1.3	1.6

Middle East

Egypt	pound	1.3	2.9	3.4	3.8
Israel	shekel	1,484	2.1*	1,729	4.1*
Saudi Arabia	riyal	3.6	3.7	3.7	3.7
Turkey	lira	579	2,874	40,390	670,300

*Readjusted in currency revaluation program.

**Euro Area countries (see *What Is the Euro?*)

8. WHAT ARE THE WORLD'S MAJOR CURRENCIES?

THE CURRENCIES OF the world have names and backgrounds that are as diverse as the countries that issue them.

The world's newest currency, the *euro* (see *What Is the Euro?*), was recently created to replace the national currencies of France, Germany, the Netherlands, Belgium, Luxembourg, Finland, Ireland, Portugal, Spain, Italy, Austria, and Greece. The "euro area" countries agreed to give up their francs, marks, and guilders and use only euros as of January 1, 2002. The euro, of course, derives its name from the continent, which got its name from Europa, a mythical wife of the Greek god Zeus.

The *dollar*, used in many English-speaking countries around the world, got its name from a silver coin minted during the Middle Ages in a small valley, or "thal," in Bohemia called Joachimsthal. Just as a sausage from Frankfurt came to be called a frankfurter, the coins from Joachimsthal were called "Joachimsthaler" or simply "thaler," and eventually came to be called "dollars" in English.

The *pound*, used in Britain, Egypt, and Lebanon, among other places, refers to the weights used in minting the currency— originally, one Roman pound (12 ounces) of silver. The word *penny* has the same origin as the word *pawn*, as in "pawn shop." It originally meant "to pledge," since a penny, like any unit of currency, is a pledge of value.

The name for currency in Turkey and in Italy before the euro is *lira*—which comes from the Latin word *libra*, meaning "pound."

In Spanish-speaking countries, the word meaning "weight," *peso,* has been used to describe a variety of coins. Originally, there were gold coins in Spain called *peso de oro,* and silver coins called *peso de plata.* The word *peso* is used to describe the currencies in many countries of Latin America, including Mexico, Argentina, and Chile.

The *franc,* used in Switzerland and Senegal—as well as in France and Belgium before the euro, is based on the early coins used in France that bore the Latin inscription *franconium rex,* meaning "king of the Franks," the Franks being one of the tribes that originally settled the area.

The German *mark* and the Finnish *markka* derived their names from the small marks that were cut into coins to indicate their precious metal content.

The *real* in Brazil, the *riyal* in Saudi Arabia and Qatar, and the *rial* in Iran are all derived from the Latin *regal(is),* referring to the royal origin of the early currencies. The *dinar,* used in Iraq and Kuwait, among other countries, derives its name from *denarius,* a Roman coin.

In India, Pakistan, and other countries neighboring the subcontinent, the currency is called *rupee.* In Indonesia it is called *rupiah.* The name comes from the Sanskrit word *rupya,* meaning "coined silver."

The name of the Japanese currency, the *yen,* and the Chinese currency, the *yuan,* are both derived from the ancient Chinese word *yiam,* meaning "round," or "small round thing."

The @ sign, used in the name of several Web-based currencies, also had its origin in the world of measurement. Clay jars, or *amphore,* were often used as a form of measurement in the countries that traded across the Mediterranean, and traders in medieval times used to draw a loop around the letters used to keep track of these amphore, turning the "a" for each amphora into an @. The first recorded use of the @ was found in a sixteenth-century letter from the written by an Italian merchant to describe the arrival in Spain of three ships bearing gold and silver from Latin America.

9. WHAT IS THE EURO?

THE WORLD'S NEWEST currency, the euro (€), was established on January 1, 1999, when eleven countries—Germany, France, Italy, Spain, Portugal, Ireland, Austria, Finland, Belgium, Luxembourg, and the Netherlands—decided to permanently abandon their national currencies and form the so-called "euro area." Even though actual euro coins and notes were only allowed to circulate after January 1, 2002, the member currencies were joined together by common consent: from that day on, none of the currencies would ever again be allowed to fluctuate against the others.

The euro had already become a virtual currency in the sense that people could open checking accounts in euros, buy euro-denominated stocks and bonds, and pay credit card bills with euros—rather than the usual French francs, German marks, or Italian lire.

The decision to install a new currency in Europe had far-reaching ramifications. In addition to facilitating trade and finance, the use of a common currency has changed the economic and fiscal landscape drastically. In one fell swoop, the national central banks, such as the Banque de France and the Deutsche Bundesbank, were rendered obsolete, and a new entity, the *European*

Central Bank (ECB), was established in Frankfurt, with full responsibility for deciding exchange rate and monetary policy in the eleven countries that made up the euro area. The ECB's governing council is made up of the central bank presidents of each member country, as well as the six members of the ECB executive board.

One of the ECB's first tasks was to deal with each member country's divergent economic priorities. Just as it's hard for the Federal Reserve to balance the needs of each region of the United States—California could be booming, for example, while the Northeast stagnates—the European Central Bank found it difficult to treat all the various countries of the European Union as a single economic zone. It was decided, therefore, to try to make the economies of the euro area converge as much as possible, especially in the areas of inflation, growth, and unemployment.

For example, Greece was the first European Union country to be refused entry into the euro area, mainly because it was unable to meet the stringent inflation and debt criteria. These criteria consist of keeping inflation below three percent and limiting government budget deficits and debt as a percentage of GDP to minimum levels. However, by the year 2000, Greece had succeeded in bringing its economy into line with the others and was allowed to join the euro area.

Sweden, Denmark, and the United Kingdom initially refused to join the bold new "experiment," as many called it. Fearful of losing control of their own monetary policy as well as losing cherished currencies, they chose a wait-and-see attitude before adopting the euro. Even though their currencies initially remained strong against the euro, they soon began having second thoughts as companies moved operations into euro-area countries to take advantage of the stable exchange rates. In

Britain, for example, several major companies announced plant closures, saying they would only return when the U.K. adopted the euro.

Most euro area members expected their new currency to quickly replace the dollar as the prime international reserve currency, pointing out that the size of the European Union's economy was already larger than that of the United States or Japan. However, for the first few years of its existence, the euro declined sharply in value against both the dollar and the yen as the world waited to see if the euro area countries could actually work together closely enough to ensure the stable monetary and economic policies essential to the currency's long-term strength.

10. WHAT IS VIRTUAL MONEY?

ALMOST ALL MONEY is virtual, in one way or another. Only coins minted in silver or gold, or some other precious commodity, are really worth anything. All other money is just a promise of value—a piece of paper with George Washington's portrait on it is like a check or an online bank account in that it is only worth what it can purchase.

Essentially, money is a promise to the seller that they will be paid—somehow, somewhere—for parting with whatever it is they're selling. As much as people want to believe a hundred-dollar bill is valuable in itself, it is only worth what other people think it will give them.

Virtual money has existed ever since someone in medieval Venice had the clever idea to invent double-ledger accounting. In order to avoid the cumbersome moving of heavy coins from one account to the other, merchants and bankers on the Rialto Bridge simply wrote down—in a big book—the credits and debits of each client. The virtual world of Web finance is just an extension of what the merchants of Venice were doing back in the Middle Ages: crediting one account and debiting another.

Originally, almost all transactions on the Web were paid for with credit cards, a form of virtual money where a number—and sometimes, a signature—is all that is needed to have a book or a box of fruit sent from one part of the world to another. Eventually other forms of payment came into use, such as charging the purchaser's phone bill or debitting the user's Internet Service Provider (ISP), which had the advantage of allowing consumers to avoid giving their credit card numbers over the Web.

Eventually, entirely new forms of Web "currencies" were invented. Some allowed people to load a certain amount of money onto their own Web accounts and then spend this virtual money online. Others involved using various services, such a PayPal.com or PayMe.com, which allowed Web users to transfer money in the form of e-mail.

Parents found they could better control their children's online purchases by providing them with pre-loaded accounts of "Web money"—instead of letting them use credit cards with unlimited purchasing power. Users of Web accounts normally make purchases by debiting virtual Web accounts, which are topped off periodically to keep them in balance.

Another alternative to using credit cards for Web purchases can be found in e-commerce cards, or eComCards, which work like prepaid telephone cards in that they are purchased—from stores, banks, or online—with a certain amount of money loaded on them. Their sixteen-digit numbers allowed them to be used on the Web like a credit card, but only for the amount originally paid for.

Some Web currency services even allow people to earn money online. By visiting certain Web sites, for example, or by filling in online surveys, clients are able to earn "virtual money," which is credited to their accounts on the Web. This money can then be used to pay for online purchases or, in some cases, converted back into "real" money. In many ways, the "click money" is similar to another form of virtual money, frequent flyer miles.

With an estimated three trillion unused air miles floating around, it was only a matter of time before someone had the idea of using them for purchases on the Web as well. Instead of only being used to buy more flights, frequent flyer miles can be used to purchase many other things on the Web, from MP3 music to Mediterranean cruises. Even at conservative real money valuations, there is more than thirty billion dollars' worth of unused frequent flyer miles virtual money waiting to be spent at any given time.

Web money, just like normal money, can be stored for later use—either on the Web itself or digitally transferred to chips embedded on cards. These "smart cards" or "chipper cards" can be used to pay for everyday purchases at terminals set up at many different "points of sale," such as grocery stores or movie theaters.

The "smart card" technology, developed in Europe during the 1990s, allows consumers to use cards embedded with an electronic chip to pay for purchases at stores and many other points of sale. Smart cards are a type of virtual money that can be used to pay for purchases through the use of a tamperproof chip that provides the store with updatable personal information. This information can usually only be accessed when the customer enters a secret PIN (Personal Identification Number).

Although similar to debit cards, which transfer money directly to the store from the cardholder's bank account, smart cards can actually have money loaded directly onto them, usually by inserting them into a bank machine or automatic teller machine (ATM).

The "money" embedded onto a smart card's chip is worth just as much in a French department store or a Dutch casino as a sack of coins. The disadvantage of this type of virtual money is that if someone loses a loaded Smart Card, they usually lose the money loaded onto the card as well. The loss is in that case not virtual at all.

11. WHAT ARE FREELY FLOATING CURRENCIES?

APART FROM A few misguided misers like Ebenezer Scrooge, no one wants a currency "to have and to hold, until death do you part." Currencies are used to buy goods and services, both at home and abroad, and their value is determined in many different ways.

It used to be that a currency's value was fixed by the government or was linked to some item of value. In the United States, for example, until 1971, dollars could be converted into gold. This *gold standard* was meant to guarantee that currencies would always have a certain value, determined by the amount of gold held in each country's vaults. This is no longer the case—at least not in the United States.

Most countries abandoned the gold standard in the 1930s,

when insufficient gold reserves forced governments to adopt a system of *fixed exchange rates* where each country's government decided on its own what its currency was going to be worth. The British government, for example, had decided that pounds would be exchanged into U.S. dollars at the rate of $2.40 per British pound. When the Smithsonian Agreement of fixed exchange rates collapsed in 1973, currencies were allowed to "float" on the international markets. One day a dollar could be worth ten Swedish kroner, the next day it could be worth eleven. From then on, the markets would decide what the world's major currencies were worth.

What determines the "price" of a currency? Just like a concert ticket on the night of a sold-out performance, a freely floating currency's price goes up when there is increased demand. It is hard to envision, but currencies are scarce commodities—just like apples or crude oil. Their price depends on supply and demand. When everyone wants to buy Japanese cars and stereo systems, for example, the "price" of yen tends to go up. This happens because importers in Paris and Minneapolis have to use their euros and dollars to buy yen to pay for the increased Japanese imports. Likewise, if all Italians decided to go on vacation in Florida, the Italian lira would eventually lose value as it is sold to buy dollars—which are then used to pay for Mickey Mouse T-shirts and Disney World admission tickets.

All of the world's major currencies—from the Swiss franc to the yen to the dollar to the euro—are traded on the world's foreign exchange, or *forex,* markets. This free-float system does not keep governments from trying to influence the value of their currencies from time to time, however. By buying or selling large amounts of currency—or by raising or lowering interest rates—a government is able to raise or lower the value of any currency. This system, sometimes called a "dirty float," is usually only a stopgap measure.

Like trying to reverse the flow of water, it is very difficult to halt the slide of a currency once traders and investors decide it is headed for a fall. Because of the enormous amount of currency traded every day on the world's foreign exchange markets—it had reached 1.5 trillion dollars by the year 2000—interventions by central banks are often just a drop in the bucket.

The values of freely floating currencies are influenced mainly by economic and political events—and sometimes by the sheer speculation of individual traders. Foreign exchange traders may bet that a currency will increase or decline in value—just as a commodities trader bets that wheat or pork bellies will go up or down at some point in the future. Basically, if interest rates look set to rise in Tokyo, meaning higher return for yen-based investments, traders may rush to sell dollars and euros and buy yen, expecting other investors to follow suit.

No one, however, knows for sure what direction currency markets are going to take. Since economic information is now immediately available to everyone in the global market, exchange rate forecasts are pure speculation. At any given point in time, about half the traders and investors in the currency markets think that a particular currency will go up, and the other half thinks it will go down. If it were any different, the side "in the know" would keep buying up a currency until it reached a new equilibrium level.

During periods of economic and political turmoil, some traders and investors turn to a particular currency as a "refuge." When political unrest threatens to erupt in the Far East, for example, traders may rush to buy hard currencies such as the Swiss franc or the U.S. dollar, which are expected to hold their value in times of trouble.

12. WHAT ARE EXCHANGE RATES?

IF EVERY COUNTRY in the world used the same currency, international trade would be made much easier. Unfortunately, this is not the case. A Scottish whiskey producer wants to be paid in British pounds and a Shanghai shirtmaker wants to be paid in Chinese yuan. But what are these currencies worth?

Currencies, just like other commodities, have a certain value. Unlike other commodities, the value of a currency has to be given in terms of other currencies. Mexican pesos have a value in U.S. dollars, which have a value in British pounds, which have a value in euros, etc.—and these *exchange rates* are constantly changing.

When a Mexican peso goes down in value against a dollar and the dollar goes down against a British pound, the peso logically has to go down against the pound. If you sit on a trading floor in any major bank or look at currency trading pages on the Web, you can see these currency *cross rates* changing hundreds of times per minute. Foreign exchange is a 24-hour market, with trading going on electronically in hundreds of financial centers around the globe, from Singapore to San Francisco and from London to São Paulo.

Banks and moneychangers watch the global forex market carefully, changing their own rates constantly to stay in line with the market. When you change money in Amsterdam or Acapulco, the exchange rate is determined by the forex market, not by a central authority.

Tourists changing money abroad will notice that there are usually two exchange rates: one for people buying a particular currency, another for people selling. This "spread" between the buy and sell rates ensures that the bank or *bureau de change* makes a small profit on each transaction. Essentially, if an indecisive traveler changes money back and forth enough times, there won't be anything left.

Using a credit card to buy goods or services abroad or using a card to get money from a foreign ATM usually provides better exchange rates because the bank at home simply changes the value of the foreign purchase into the home currency using the foreign exchange rate of the day the transaction is booked—as well as adding a small fee. Global consumers can check these rates by consulting certain Web pages (such as www.oanda.com), which provide exchange rates for any given day and for almost any given currency in the world.

13. WHAT IS GNP/GDP?

IN EVERY COUNTRY in the world—from Cuba to Kuwait and from Japan to Jamaica—it is the production of goods and services that allows people to survive and prosper. Some countries may be better at producing certain goods or services, and others may have an abundance of raw materials. By selling some of its goods and services abroad, a country can increase its total economic output enormously.

Gross Domestic Product (GDP) is the term economists use to describe the total amount of goods and services produced by a country in any given year. Putting a U.S. dollar value on these goods and services is not the only way to measure the world's many different economies, but it's the easiest way to compare the value of all the apples and oranges, football games and televisions sets, movies and college classes that each economy produces.

COUNTRY		GDP IN LOCAL CURRENCY	GDP IN U.S. DOLLARS
United States	dollars	8,710,000,000,000	$8,710,000,000,000
Japan	yen	499,162,125,000,000	$4,395,000,000,000
Germany	euros	2,240,499,515,556	$2,081,200,000,000
France	euros	1,517,924,426,741	$1,410,000,000,000
United Kingdom	pounds	928,170,822,352	$1,373,600,000,000
Italy	euros	1,238,023,468,618	$1,150,000,000,000
China	yuan	8,246,275,470,000	$996,300,000,000
Brazil	reals	1,551,539,700,000	$791,400,000,000
Canada	dollars	925,894,800,000	$612,000,000,000
Mexico	pesos	4,598,160,000,000	$483,000,000,000
India	rupees	20,852,550,000,000	$447,000,000,000
Russia	rubles	5,184,016,000,000	$184,000,000,000
Indonesia	rupiahs	1,426,950,000,000,000	$151,000,000,000
Israel	sheckels	402,633,000,000	$99,000,000,000

Source: The World Bank (www.worldbank.org), 1999; and *Financial Times*.

A wider measure of economic activity, called *Gross National Product* (GNP), factors in the *international* activities of a country's residents. This may be income from foreign stocks or interest payments on bonds that the government has sold to foreigners. GNP even factors in, or out, the domestic production of goods and services from companies that are owned by foreigners. For this reason, a country such as Ireland, which has a large portion of domestic companies in foreigners' hands, has a smaller GNP than GDP. British residents and companies, on the contrary, own a lot of companies abroad, so the British Gross National Product is usually larger—because it includes foreign production that is not included in its Gross Domestic Product.

Although both figures are interesting, most economists prefer to use GDP to look at a country's economic health. Just as a speedometer is used to measure the speed of a car, GDP provides the clearest measure of a country's total economic activity.

14. HOW ARE THE WORLD'S ECONOMIES COMPARED?

IF A SMALL COUNTRY like Ireland or Sri Lanka were to win most of the gold medals at the Summer Olympics, it would certainly mean more than a victory by a large country like China or the United States. In the same way, it is difficult to evaluate the economic achievements of any country without looking at its size and the resources at its disposal.

What does it mean to say that the United States spends more money on its military than Israel? If Israel's population and economy is only a fraction of the size of the United States', comparing gross figures between the two countries is hardly useful. To compare economic statistics, therefore, it is necessary to relate them to the size of each country's population and economy. By relating military spending to the number of people living in Israel, it becomes apparent that Israel actually spends much more, per capita, on its military than the United States.

Likewise, by saying that the United States gives more foreign aid than any other country is deceiving. When you compare foreign aid to the size of the economy, measured either by GDP or GNP, it is possible to see that the United States gives much less—as a percentage of the total economy—than smaller countries such as Denmark, Sweden, and Canada.

A further problem in comparing economic statistics is the use of foreign currencies. If Japan's GDP totals 350 trillion yen and the United State's GDP is eight trillion dollars, which one is bigger? Obviously, the totals from each country have to be translated into a common currency. However, current exchange rates often give a misleading figure for the size of each country's economy, especially in low-cost countries of the Third World. A haircut in Mexico, for example, is seen in dollar terms to be worth much less than a haircut in the United States.

How do we compare the value of goods and services without using current exchange rates? Most economists prefer to use a "real world" exchange rate that is based on the value of a "basket" of goods and services in each country (see *How Is Wealth Determined Around the World?* for a more in-depth discussion of Purchasing Power Parity—PPP). Comparing different countries' GDP's by using Purchasing Power Parity often gives us a much better idea of the "true" size of each country's economy.

China's GDP, for example, is only worth a little more than a trillion dollars if measured by the simple dollar value of each good and service produced in the economy, ranking it about tenth in the world. But when the PPP exchange rate is used, which adjusts for the lower dollar value of most goods and services in the Chinese economy, the total economic output is estimated to be almost four trillion dollars—ranking China's GDP as second in the world, just behind the United States.

In order to determine each person's share of the country's total economic output, raw GDP and GNP numbers need to be divided by the number of people living in each country. This allows us to compare economic statistics between countries of different sizes. Looking at GDP per capita, and adjusting it for purchasing power parity allows us to see what each person really has—on average—in any given economy:

Country	GDP (IN U.S. DOLLARS. ADJUSTED FOR PPP) GDP	GDP PER CAPITA (IN U.S. DOLLARS. ADJUSTED FOR PPP).
United States	$9,255,000,000,000	$33,900
China	$4,800,000,000,000	$3,800
Japan	$2,950,000,000,000	$23,400
Germany	$1,864,000,000,000	$22,700
India	$1,805,000,000,000	$1,800
France	$1,373,000,000,000	$23,300
United Kingdom	$1,290,000,000,000	$21,800
Italy	$1,212,000,000,000	$21,400
Brazil	$1,057,000,000,000	$6,150
Canada	$722,300,000,000	$23,300
Russia	$620,000,000,000	$2,800
Indonesia	$610,000,000,000	$2,800
Israel	$105,400,000,000	18,300

Source: *The World Factbook 2000*; the Central Intelligence Agency (www.cia.gov)

Comparing countries by looking at their GDP can by misleading in that neither GDP nor GNP completely measures the size of a country's total economy. Illegal activities, such as drug sales or prostitution, are never reported and are consequently not included in the "official" measures. In addition, work done for no salary, such as housework, subsistence farming, or volunteer work at schools and hospitals, is not included, since no payment is made for these goods or services. A country with many dual-income families would consequently show an "inflated" GDP, reflecting the added costs of day care and cleaning services previously provided "for free" by a stay-at-home spouse.

Although neither GDP nor GNP is a perfect measure, they still provide the best means we have to see the size of a country's total economy—and consequently are useful in comparing the economic activities of countries around the world, big and small.

15. WHAT IS MONEY SUPPLY?

EVEN AN "ECONOMY" as small as a Monopoly game is controlled by its money supply. If more Monopoly money is made available to each player, more property, houses, and hotels can be bought, making the game much more exciting.

Every economy in the world is based on the use of money. Therefore, each country's money supply determines how quickly the economy can grow. If the central bank increases the money supply, consumers and businesses have more money to spend on goods and services.

Just as the game of Monopoly can be stimulated by increasing the amount of money available to its players, a country can encourage economic growth by increasing its money supply, which includes currency in circulation and readily available funds such as bank deposits on which checks can be drawn. This "narrow" measure is usually called "M1" because it refers to the first level of money supply. This is easy-to-access money, often called "high-powered" money because it is the money used for most consumer and business expenditures. When consumers get a tax refund deposited into their bank accounts, their first reaction is usually to go out and spend it.

Other wider measures of money supply—such as M2, M3, etc.—include funds that are not so readily available, such as time deposits and other long-term investments.

Basically, when businesses and individuals have less money at their disposal, economic activity slows. Central banks often limit money supply growth (see following section) in order to slow down the economy and control inflation. In a Monopoly game, when less money is floating around the board, players will be less freewheeling with their property purchases. On the larger scale of a national economy, a tightening at the central bank leads to reduced money supply growth, which usually translates into an economic downturn.

Conversely, the money supply can be increased to stimulate economic activity. If the players in a Monopoly game are given more than two hundred dollars for passing Go, for example, the results are predictable: the "economy" speeds up and players start buying properties from each other at higher and higher prices. Increasing the economy's money supply almost always results in rapid growth and inflated prices.

16. WHAT IS INFLATION?

IT USED TO be that reports of a surging economy brought euphoria to its markets. When factories were producing at full capacity and people all had jobs, the markets would greet the news with approval, confident that in a booming economy everyone would be better off.

However, after the severe inflation scares of the past decades, with prices rising out of control in some countries, leaders have realized that an economy that is growing too quickly could be too much of a good thing. When unemployment falls, companies are forced to pay higher wages for scarce workers and prices of goods and services need to be raised to pay for the increased cost. Inflation, even in so-called New Economies, is now the "Public Enemy Number One" of most economic decision-makers.

Each country keeps track of inflation by looking at the

prices of a "basket," or group of goods and services, that is chosen to reflect the lifestyles of the average person. This basket is constantly being updated—adding computers and Internet services in the industrialized countries, for example—to accurately reflect what it costs to live in any given economy. In the United States, this measure is called the *consumer price index* (CPI). In Britain, it is called the *retail price index* (RPI).

Inflation is usually defined as the percentage rise in the costs of the chosen basket of goods and services over a given period of time. Deflation, a decline in prices, rarely occurs because most companies are reluctant to cut prices, even when the costs of production go down, and most employees would quit their jobs if their salaries were reduced. *Disinflation,* not to be confused with deflation, is simply a decline in the rate of inflation.

In a booming economy, even one with high-technology fueling rapid growth in productivity, inflation begins to rise as soon as consumers and businesses compete for increasingly scarce goods and services. It's a chicken-or-the-egg scenario: employees ask for higher salaries to pay the higher prices, and companies, forced to hire increasingly expensive labor, are forced to raise prices to cover their increased costs. The result is often a vicious circle of wage and price increases that end up hurting almost everyone—especially those on fixed incomes who see their buying power decline when their incomes are not adjusted for the rise in prices.

Normally, when governments and central banks see the first signs of inflation (see following section), they try to slow down the economy. They "put on the brakes" by increasing interest rates, which makes almost all activities, such as buying a new car on credit or building a new factory, more expensive. Higher interest rates usually end up reducing business and consumer spending, which leads to a reduction in employment and a slowdown in the economy.

The international markets watch each country's inflation rate carefully—always looking for signs that an economy is not overheating. International investors, including gigantic pension funds and banks, move billions and sometimes trillions of dollars, euros, and yen around the world on any given day, looking for the best return on their investment. When a country's economy looks like it is growing too strongly, and it looks as if inflation is about to rear its ugly head, international investors can move their money out at a moment's notice (see *What Is Hot Money?* and *What Is Hyperinflation?*), preferring to invest their money in countries with stable economic growth and low inflation rates.

17. WHAT IS A CENTRAL BANK?

JUST AS A prudent driver keeps an eye on the road ahead and a steady hand on the wheel, a country's central bank tries to keep the economy on course. A central bank looks at economic data such as factory orders, housing, consumer credit, retail sales, manufacturing, and construction and employment figures in an effort to keep the economy from overheating. It consequently adjusts money supply and interest rates to keep the economy headed in the right direction.

Instead of taking deposits and making loans like a normal bank, a central bank—such as the U.S. Federal Reserve or the Bank of Japan—controls the economy principally by increasing or decreasing the country's supply of money. Cranking up the printing presses, however, is not the main way a central bank increases the country's money supply (see *How Do Central Banks Regulate an Economy?*). In most modern economies, printed notes and coins are only a small percentage—usually less than ten percent—of the total money supply. Central banks print only enough currency to satisfy the everyday needs of business and consumers. In the United States, the Federal Reserve usually prints up only enough bills to replace worn-out money in circulation.

But a central bank is much more than a national piggy bank. Besides coordinating a country's monetary policy, the central bank serves as a watchdog, supervising the country's banking and financial system. In most countries, the central bank is given a considerable degree of independence. In the United States, for example, the president appoints the head of the Federal Reserve, but from that moment on, the government has no significant say in how the money supply is regulated.

The activities and responsibilities of central banks vary widely from country to country. The Bank of England, for example, is responsible for printing the money as well as supervising the banking system and coordinating monetary policy. The European Central Bank head oversees the monetary policy for all the countries in the euro area, but is limited in how much it can intervene in each country.

In the United States, central bank duties are divided among several different agencies: the U.S. Treasury borrows money for the government's use by issuing Treasury notes and bonds, while the Federal Reserve Board charts monetary policy and oversees the printing of money at the Bureau of Printing and Engraving.

The Bank of Japan, like many other central banks, acts as

a banker to the government, issuing the government's checks and holding its deposits of foreign currency. Some central banks, such as the Swiss National Bank, are partly owned by private shareholders.

During times of financial panic, central banks often act as a "lender of last resort," in order to preserve the stability of the country's financial system. In times of international crisis, central banks sometimes turn to their own central bank, the Bank for International Settlements (BIS), based in Basel, Switzerland. In addition to advising and supervising the international banking community, the BIS sometimes provides temporary funds to shore up failing banking systems around the world. The BIS usually provides only short-term financing called *bridge loans,* which are paid back as soon as longer-term financing can be arranged.

As its name implies, the Bank for International Settlements is also used to transfer funds from one central bank to another. The Federal Reserve may use the BIS to facilitate a payment to the Bank of Japan, or the Mexican Central Bank may use the BIS to transfer money to China. Just like cashing a check at a local bank, the key for these international transfers is to have one central "clearing" authority that credits one account and debits another. No actual money ever changes hands—it doesn't have to, as long as the central bank keeps track of payments.

18. HOW DO CENTRAL BANKS REGULATE AN ECONOMY?

UNLIKE DONALD DUCK'S miserly Uncle Scrooge, most people don't store their savings in a big vault at home. They put their money in banks, where it is made available to the economy at large.

Since most money in any economy is in the form of bank deposits, the most efficient way for a central bank to regulate the economy is to regulate bank lending and bank deposits. When banks have more money to lend to customers, the economy grows. When banks reduce lending, the economy slows.

It works like this: when a customer deposits money in a bank, it doesn't just sit there. The bank lends the money to someone else. A hundred dollars deposited in a bank in Albuquerque, for example, may end up being loaned to a business in Santa Fe. After setting aside a small portion of each deposit as a "reserve," banks lend out the remainder. The effect is to increase the money supply without any new currency being printed. This is referred to by economists as a "multiplier effect" in that bank lending can increase the money supply well beyond the amount of money actually printed.

A bank's supply of money for lending is limited only by the amount of its deposits and by its *reserve requirements,* which are determined by the central bank. Most banks are required to put a certain percentage of their funds—10 percent of deposits, for example—on reserve with the central bank and are, therefore, unable to lend these funds back to customers.

When a central bank increases the reserve requirement, it

effectively reduces the money supply: banks have less to lend to businesses and consumers. On the other hand, by reducing the reserve requirements, a central bank allows the banks to lend more. Because of the enormous amount of money loaned by banks to the economy at large, altering reserve requirements has become one of the most effective tools used by central banks to control the money supply.

Central banks can also control the money supply by raising or lowering interest rates (see *How Are Interest Rates Used to Control Economic Growth?*). When a central bank decides an economy is growing too slowly, it reduces the interest rate it charges on its loans to banks, which results in cheaper loans to businesses and consumers. Alternatively, if an economy shows signs of growing too quickly, a central bank can increase the interest rates on its loans to banks, reducing the available supply of money and putting the brakes on economic growth.

Perhaps the most dramatic way of increasing or decreasing the money supply is through *open market operations,* where a central bank buys or sells large amounts of securities, such as government treasury bonds, in the open market. By buying a large block of bonds from a bank or securities house, the central bank is, in effect, pumping money into the economy, freeing up funds that were not previously part of the money supply. This money then becomes available for banks to lend out to consumers and businesses.

In a sense, the central bank "creates" money every time it dips into its vaults to buy bonds in the open market. Whether it pays by check or cash, or simply credits the bank's account, a central bank is injecting new money into the economy every time it buys bonds on the open market. Just like the bank in the game of Monopoly, a central bank, unlike other players in the economy, does not have to secure funding from any other source.

Conversely, when a central bank sells bonds in the open market, it reduces the money supply. The payments from banks and securities houses for the bonds sold enter the "black hole" of the central bank's vaults—where money is completely removed from the economy at large.

The "New Economy" has presented central banks, and the Fed in particular, with a whole new set of variables. The enormous productivity growth in some countries, in part based on technological advances, has created a new paradigm—a new set of rules by which to judge economic growth. The rapid expansion of the U.S. economy in the late 1990s, for example, was more than double the rate over the previous twenty-five years. Even though the unemployment rate was hovering around four percent, there were still no signs of inflation to prompt the Fed to raise interest rates.

Monetary policy is a difficult guessing game, and central bankers are often called upon to make important decisions without knowing exactly where the economy is heading. If the central bank allows the economy to expand too rapidly by keeping too much money in circulation, it may cause unwanted inflation. If it slows down the economy by removing too much money from circulation, an economic recession can result, bringing unemployment and reduced production. An error in judgment at the central bank has grave consequences for everyone in the economy.

19. HOW ARE INTEREST RATES USED TO CONTROL ECONOMIC GROWTH?

IN FREE-MARKET economies, consumers and businesses can do almost anything they want with money—as long as they pay for it. Therefore, by controlling interest rates—the "cost" of money—central banks can greatly influence economic activity.

In a totalitarian country, the government can simply tell its citizens what it wants them to do: today you will buy bread, tomorrow you will not. But in free-market countries, consumers and businesses are encouraged to increase or reduce their economic activity through economic incentives.

For example, when a central bank decides that an economy is growing too slowly—or not growing at all—it reduces the interest rate it charges on its loans to banks. When banks get "cheaper" money at the central bank, they can make cheaper loans to businesses and consumers, providing an important stimulus to economic growth. Likewise, by raising interest rates, a central bank can slow down an economy. When interest rates go up, people don't buy as many houses, cars, and restaurant meals—and economic activity declines.

Since most banks borrow money from the central bank, the interest rate the central bank charges affects further lending throughout the economy. When a central bank changes its *discount rate,* the interest rate it charges for loans to banks, interest rates across the economy almost always follow suit. The interest rates on loans made between banks—called *interbank rates* in Europe and *Fed Funds rates* in the United States—logically will rise whenever banks have to pay more to borrow from central banks. The higher cost of money is almost always passed on to consumers and businesses in the form of higher interest rates—on credit card debt or home loans, for example.

All interest rates are linked, of course, because money, like most commodities, is interchangeable. Banks and individuals will go wherever rates are lowest—basically, wherever money is cheapest. A change in interest rates by the Fed in Washington will not only affect interest rates in Los Angeles, but will often affect interest rates around the world. In the global village of the international money markets, interest rates have become the heartbeat of economic activity.

20. WHAT IS FREE TRADE?

WITH THE LEVEL playing field of open markets, companies in one country are forced to compete with companies in other countries to sell their goods and services. When every country in the world is allowed to do what it does best— letting the French excel in fashion, for example, or the Japanese in consumer electronics, or the Americans in aircraft and movies—the world economy prospers.

The downside is that free trade exposes local producers to foreign competition, which can be hard on inefficient or poorly managed companies. This can lead to short-term layoffs and idle factories, a disaster for small towns that rely on a local industry for jobs and tax revenue.

But nothing in the fast-changing global economy stays the same for long. Confronted with foreign competition, many local companies take the necessary steps to become more efficient, thus enabling them in the end to compete and prosper at home as well as abroad. Others, however, call for "managed" trade, a return to some restrictions on foreign products. Others simply prefer an outright ban on imports (see *What Are Quotas, Tariffs, and Subsidies?*).

If a government wants to encourage trade with another country, the first step is to remove restrictions to its internal markets. This courtesy, previously called "most favored nation status" in the United States, is now referred to as *Permanent Normal Trade Relations* (PNTR). The idea is that barriers to trade are eventually eliminated in both countries. The decision to grant China PNTR in the year 2000, for example, not only removed U.S. restrictions on Chinese-made goods, but called for the Chinese to abolish import quotas and licenses on U.S. goods and services, immediately reducing average tariffs from 24 percent to 9 percent.

When a country wants to encourage exports, it tries to find incentives that will make its products more competitive on the world markets. Some countries provide loans or grants to foreign buyers of a country's goods and services through *export-import banks*. These state-supported "ex-im" banks often provide low-cost loans, called *export subsidies,* to stimulate sales of goods and services abroad.

Countries may also encourage trade by allowing *barter* between local companies and companies from economies that are experiencing currency problems. For example, in some Eastern European countries, bartering may involve trading a shipment of Pepsi-Cola for a shipment of vodka, or a truckload of computers for a tanker full of oil. Bartering often allows countries to overcome a temporary shortage of "hard" foreign currencies, such as dollars or euros.

Sometimes, a country might want to encourage imports of

foreign goods and services in order to decrease international tensions resulting from large trade imbalances. For example, when Japan was criticized for running large trade surpluses, particularly by the United States, it decided to stimulate the purchase of foreign goods.

One of the most effective tools for stimulating imports is to increase the value of a country's currency. This can be done, in the short term at least, through government intervention on the international foreign-exchange markets. The goal is to make foreign goods and services less expensive than locally made products, thereby stimulating imports. This process is sometimes referred to as *external adjustment*.

A country may also encourage imports by stimulating its economy through lower interest rates, thus increasing overall spending on foreign goods such as automobiles or luxury goods. In countries such as Germany and France, where many consumer goods are imported, lowering interest rates can encourage imports of everything from Brazilian shoes to Canadian snow boards.

Another way to encourage imports is to reduce cultural barriers to trade. The Japanese government, for example, has tried in the past to encourage consumers to overcome their reluctance to buy anything foreign. In some cases, the government has encouraged purchases of everything from German automobiles to U.S. beef. The goal, of course, is not to hurt local producers, but to forestall threats of retaliatory sanctions from uneasy trading partners.

21. WHAT ARE QUOTAS, TARIFFS, AND SUBSIDIES?

ALTHOUGH A TRADE war may not be as destructive as a military war, in both cases many people suffer—often the very people the war was meant to protect.

By attempting to protect a few jobs in inefficient industries, trade restrictions often force consumers and businesses to buy poorly made and relatively expensive domestic products. For example, it is estimated that U.S. restrictions on imports of cheap foreign steel during the 1990s, while protecting a few thousand jobs at inefficient American steel manufacturers, ended up costing U.S. consumers and businesses billions of dollars in increased costs for everything from refrigerators to minivans.

The most common trade barriers are quotas, tariffs, and subsidies. By imposing a *quota,* a country limits the quantity of foreign products that can be imported. A *tariff* is a tax placed on goods entering a country, raising the price of foreign-made goods. Governments can also use taxpayers' money to provide a *subsidy* to local producers, making the price of local goods artificially lower than imported goods.

Trade barriers, like walls between feuding neighbors, are usually imposed unilaterally by one country acting on its own to limit imports. These barriers are usually designed to "temporarily" protect local producers from foreign competition and allow them time to improve their productivity. The problem is that local producers, once given the comfort of a protected market, rarely make the sacrifices necessary to improve their products or lower their prices.

22. WHAT IS THE WTO?

WHEN A COUNTRY unilaterally erects trade barriers, other countries often follow suit, putting up trade barriers of their own, which can escalate into full-scale trade wars, or, even worse, military conflict. During the 1930s, for example, the United States' decision to put up trade barriers ended up leading to a worldwide depression—and, some say, World War II.

Every country wants free access to the world's markets, but at the same time, many governments try to protect local producers from the demands of foreign competition. Even though consumers and businesses almost always benefit from unlimited access to imports, political pressure from an inefficient industry is sometimes too great for a government to resist.

To resolve trade disputes, governments often "barter" free trade, agreeing to only remove a barrier to a specific import when other countries remove barriers of their own. This is a bit of a paradox: even though governments around the world know that free trade is a win-win situation, they still insist on making the removal of trade barriers a "tit for tat" process.

Once free-trade agreements are in place, some sort of mechanism is needed to ensure that countries respect their promises. The closest thing the world has to a trade "watchdog" is the World Trade Organization (WTO). Like its predecessor, the General Agreement on Tariffs and Trade (GATT), the World Trade Organization is based in Geneva, Switzerland. The WTO's mandate is simple: when two or more countries have a dispute, they ask the WTO to help them resolve it peacefully.

Despite the fact that the WTO is blamed for a wide variety

of ills in modern society, it can be argued that its role was never intended to be more than a round table around which disputing parties could meet to air their grievances. In fact, the WTO has no power to force any country to do anything against its own national interests. Its only form of "punishment" is to permit the country that has suffered illegal trade barriers to erect trade barriers of its own—usually in the form of tariffs. For example, when it was determined that the American economy suffered from the European Union's refusal to allow unrestricted banana imports, the U.S. was allowed to impose tariffs on a wide range of EU goods, including Roquefort cheese and Italian truffles. These *punitive tariffs* are usually meant to allow a damaged country to make up for the losses caused by the "guilty" party.

In the end, most countries find it is in their own best interest to stay within the WTO framework, even if they do not agree with all of its decisions. Of course, a country can always choose to drop out at any time, but it runs the risk of cutting itself off from the benefits, as well as the drawbacks, of free trade.

The WTO has also been criticized by protesters in rich countries for not taking stronger stands to protect the environment or labor standards, especially in the poor countries of the world. On the other hand, poor countries criticize the WTO for catering to these rich country demands for stricter environmental and labor standards, because they see these demands as just another way of refusing them access to the world economy. Many developing country leaders point out that they simply can't afford the expensive technology to ensure pollution-free production.

Supporters of the WTO point out that it is essentially just a forum to resolve trade disputes—and that several other bodies already exist to resolve issues related to the environment and labor standards. The United Nations, for example, is often used to resolve disputes over environmental protection, and the International Labor Organization (ILO), based in Geneva, was set up precisely to oversee world labor standards and guarantee fair working conditions for workers around the world. The World Health Organization (WHO), also based in Geneva, was set up by the United Nations to oversee global health issues, including the effect of public health on the world economy.

The WTO does sometimes consider environmental health and workers' rights in making its decisions. In the late 1990s, for example, the WTO allowed France to ban the imports of asbestos from Canada because of health concerns. Like everything else in the world economy, the decision had far-reaching consequences. The French were able to boost local production of substitute products, but the Canadian asbestos mining industry, employing thousands of people, had to eliminate jobs.

In the end, almost all trade decisions have undesirable consequences. Dismantling the world trading system, however, would end up hurting everyone—especially those people in the poorest countries who look to free markets as their only hope to grow their way out of poverty and economic isolation.

23. WHO INVESTS IN THE GLOBAL MARKETPLACE?

ANYONE WHO INVESTS in the global marketplace does so for one of three reasons: speculation, hedging, or arbitrage.

Most investors in the international markets are *specula-*

tors in that they believe that the market is going to move in a certain direction—and they buy or sell based on that belief. A Dutch pension fund, for example, invests money in Australian gold mines, hoping to profit from higher commodity prices. A little old lady in Poughkeepsie, New York, invests money in dotcom stocks, hoping to make a killing if the markets boom again. In fact, there is no way to know what will actually happen and speculators never all agree on anything. For every buyer, there is almost always—at the right price—a seller.

Essentially, speculators take a risk. If the market moves in the right direction, they make a profit. If not, they lose. Other players in the global markets—*hedgers* and *arbitrageurs,* balance the frenzied activity of speculators.

Hedgers have no idea where prices will go; they only know they want to protect themselves from unwanted moves in the markets. An elderly Canadian retiree, for example, buys a house as a hedge against inflation—assuming that the house's value will go up as prices in general rise. Exporters also become hedgers when they buy currency options to lock in the value of a foreign currency, guaranteeing a profit in their home currency even before the goods have been paid for.

The basic role of a hedger is to remove risk by making investments that balance potential losses.

Arbitrageurs, on the other hand, try to take advantage of discrepancies in the market. An arbitrageur will buy in one market, where prices are cheap, and sell in another where prices are more expensive. A German tourist may try to take advantage of price and currency differences by buying German-made CDs in Hong Kong and then selling them to friends back in Hamburg.

True arbitrageurs take no risk when they are able to buy in one market and sell in another at the same time. An arbitrageur takes advantage of market discrepancies, wherever they may be.

The term arbitrageur is also sometimes used to describe takeover specialists who buy and sell undervalued companies.

Generally markets are made more efficient by the disparate activities of speculators, hedgers, and arbitrageurs. One couldn't exist without the other. If the market consisted only of farmers trying to get rid of a bumper wheat crop, the prices might drop precipitously. Speculators and arbitrageurs keep the market from becoming a one-way street by buying or selling whenever prices move too far in one direction or are out of line with prices in other markets around the world.

24. WHAT IS EQUITY?

OWNERSHIP IN A company, called equity, used to be certified by pieces of paper called shares, or stock. Today, most stock is issued—and traded—electronically. But the concept is the same: the owner of equity has a share of a company.

Basically, a stockholder owns a piece of the company. When the company makes a big profit, its owners share in the benefits—usually by receiving a dividend, a payment made to all the shareholders, or by seeing the price of the company's stock rise if the profits are retained within the company.

Like all ownership, there are risks involved in equity investment. The value of the company can go down, sometimes drastically. When a company loses a lot of money, dividends are reduced or eliminated and the share's price usually falls. In the worst case, the company goes bankrupt. The shares then become worthless and the owners lose everything.

An equity investment is generally considered to be riskier than a bond. In contrast to the "fixed income" of a bond, the return on an equity investment is unknown. To reward investors for this risk, equity tends to provide a higher return over the long term—either as dividend payments or as an increase in the value of the shares, or both. Someone investing a thousand dollars in the stocks that make up the Standard & Poor's 500 Index, for example, would have seen an average return of ten percent per year over the last century—much higher than the average return on fixed-income securities. Basically, bondholders are creditors, with a guaranteed return on their investment, whereas shareholders are owners, with all the risks and rewards that ownership entails.

International equity investment is not limited to the major financial centers in London, New York, or Tokyo. An international equity investor can now buy a share of a lightbulb factory in Budapest, a Ping-Pong ball factory in Malaysia, or an oil company in Mexico. Equity means ownership, and ownership is now allowed in almost every country in the world.

25. WHY ARE COMPANIES REFERRED TO AS LTD., INC., GMBH, OR S.A.?

THE HEART OF capitalism is private ownership, and limited-liability companies allow people to own almost anything—from skyscrapers to radio stations—without risking their personal assets should the company go bankrupt.

When an entrepreneur begins a new company, it is not a

big problem to retain total responsibility and liability. But once an enterprise starts to grow, a new structure, such as a partnership or company, is required. Apple Computer founder Steven Jobs, for example, may have started out in his garage, but he soon needed the structure of a registered company. There are many risks involved in starting a business, and no one wants to see their personal savings wiped out if the enterprise fails.

The key factor in owning a share of a company is the guarantee that the owners will never have to pay more than they have invested. This is referred to as "limited liability." If a limited-liability company goes bankrupt, the owners will never be required to pay its unpaid bills. The worst that can happen to the investors is that they lose their initial investment if the company fails.

By limiting the downside risk for shareholders, companies are able to attract *equity investors* and raise large amounts of money. These funds, referred to as *equity capital,* are usually obtained by selling shares in the company instead of borrowing money at potentially high interest rates.

The names of companies around the world reflect this guarantee of limited liability. The abbreviations "S.A." in Mexico, "Ltd." in Canada, "GmbH" in Germany, and "Inc." in the United States indicate that the firm is a legal entity that can go bankrupt without forcing the shareholders to pay its debts. The "S.A." in French-speaking and Spanish-speaking countries refers to the words *Société Anonyme* or *Sociedad Anónima,* which imply the same concept as "limited." Defining the shareholders as "anonymous" means that the creditors of a bankrupt company have no right to pursue them for the company's unpaid debts.

Many countries around the world make a clear distinction between large and small companies. Generally, "public" companies are large enough to have their shares traded on recognized stock exchanges or have a large portion of their shares in public hands. Smaller companies, usually those with their shares in the hands of a small group of investors, are referred to as "private" or "unlisted" companies. In Britain, for example, Public Limited Companies, Plc's., are much bigger than Limited Companies (Ltd.). In the United States, where little distinction is made between public and private companies, most corporations simply bear the title "Incorporated," or Inc.

COMPANIES AROUND THE WORLD

Countries	Type of Company (If Applicable)	Abbreviation	Definition
United States		Inc.	Incorporated
Britain, Canada	Public	Plc.	Public Limited Company
	Private	Ltd.	Limited
France, Belgium	Public	S.A.	Société Anonyme
	Private	Sarl	Société à responsabilité limitée
Spain, Mexico, etc.		S.A.	Sociedad Anónima
Brazil, Portugal		S.A.	Sociedade Anônima
Japan		Ltd.	Limited
Germany	Public	A.G.	Aktiengesellschaft
	Private	GmbH	Gesellschaft mit beschränkte Haftung
Netherlands	Public	N.V.	Naamloze Vennootschap
	Private	B.V.	Besloten Vennootschap
Denmark		A/S	Aktieselskab
Italy	Public	SpA	Società per Azioni
	Private	Srl	Società a responsabilità limitata

26. WHAT IS A BALANCE SHEET?

IF A COCONUT juice stand on a Samoan island beach were treated as a company, its balance sheet would look like this: the *assets* would be made up of some coconuts, a knife to cut them, and any cash that happened to be on hand. If anything had been borrowed to set up the operation, these debts would be listed as *liabilities*. Whatever was left over—after subtracting the debts from the assets—would belong to the owner. This difference would be referred to as the entrepreneur's *stockholders' equity*.

BALANCE SHEET
GILLIGAN'S COCONUT JUICE INC.
(Samoan Islands)

ASSETS		LIABILITIES	
Cash:		Debts:	
$10 in coins	$10		
Inventory:		Borrowed knife	$10
10 coconuts	$10	Borrowed table	$20
Fixed Assets:		TOTAL LIABILITIES:	$30
Knife, Table	$80		
TOTAL ASSETS:	$100	Stockholder's Equity:	$70

If you want to know what a company looks like at any given point in time, you simply list all the assets and liabilities. This list, called a *balance sheet,* is essentially a snapshot of the company's financial health. Any company, even a small coconut stand in the South Pacific or a big "nonprofit" organization like the United Nations, can be understood by looking at its balance sheet.

On the left side of the balance sheet, the company lists everything it owns, such as cash and fixed assets, which are usually referred to as *property, plant, and equipment.* This list of assets can include everything from buildings to receivables to coffee machines. On the right, the company lists everything it owes. Basically, liabilities consist of all claims to the company's assets from creditors and from the company's owners. The two lists end up being exactly equal; any assets that cannot be claimed by the company's creditors belong to the owners.

When a company's shareholders sit down to see what they own, they simply subtract the company's liabilities from its assets. The shareholders then calculate the stockholders' equity, often called *book value.* This tells you what the company is worth once all the debts have been paid off.

When liabilities, such as loans from banks, rise too much, they may start to exceed the level of the company's assets. Shareholders may become nervous and sell their shares. They do not want to be around on the day when the company can no longer pay its debts and is forced to declare bankruptcy.

27. WHAT IS A PROFIT AND LOSS STATEMENT?

ANY ENTERPRISE, FROM a major conglomerate in Brazil to a small kibbutz in Israel, needs a summary of what the company has earned and spent over a given period of time. This overview of a company's activities is called an income statement or, more commonly, a *Profit and Loss statement* (P&L).

A coconut juice stand in Samoa, for example, would start

its P&L with a summary of all the money that came in, called *revenue*.

PROFIT AND LOSS STATEMENT

GILLIGAN'S COCONUT JUICE INC.
(SAMOAN ISLANDS)
PERIOD: ONE YEAR

Revenues (from sale of juice):	$500
Cost of Goods Sold (paid to Coconut Pickers):	$100
Other Expenses (advertising on beach):	$100
Gross Profit:	$300
Taxes (33.3%):	$100
Net Profit:	$200

To determine the profit, the proverbial bottom line, the company would subtract its expenses from its revenues. This is done by first subtracting the costs incurred in producing whatever it is the company made. This is referred to as *cost of goods sold*. Expenses such as salaries or maintenance of assets would then have to be accounted for. Finally, other expenses, such as interest on loans or advertising, would then be deducted.

Finally, *depreciation,* the decline in value of fixed assets such as cars and computers would have to be deducted from the earnings. This causes many accounting nightmares, because it is difficult to determine how much a fixed asset really declines in value over time. How much is your computer worth today? Certainly less than what you paid for it. But how much less?

Many companies take advantage of this uncertainty to show as much "loss" as possible in the early years of an asset's life. This allows them to reduce earnings, and pay fewer taxes, earlier rather than later. Delaying tax payments means the com-

pany can get the use of the money, including valuable interest payments if the money is invested, for a longer period of time.

Once all the expenses have been deducted from the revenues, the company can see its total profit or loss.

The P&L statement tells us how much the company's assets and liabilities have changed over the course of time. Essentially, a P&L is the link between two balance sheets. It tells what a company has done with its assets and liabilities.

Another way of understanding a company's activity over a given period of time is to look at its *cash flow.* This is similar to a P&L, except that it only measures the actual flow of funds in and out of the company during a given period of time. A company's cash flow, or "cash summary," factors out all of the accounting tricks and looks mainly at what a company really earned. Even though cash flow does not show us the company's profit, per se, it sometimes gives a clearer picture of a company's true earnings, because it excludes the hard-to-quantify items such as depreciation.

Cash flow statements, like profit and loss statements, are essential for understanding the financial health of any organization, including nonprofits such as Greenpeace or the United Nations. Even if profits are not distributed to shareholders, any organization needs to know whether it has been profitable or not.

28. WHAT IS NET WORTH?

AN INDIVIDUAL'S *NET WORTH* is calculated by adding up the monetary value of all assets, such as houses and bank accounts, and subtracting liabilities, such as mortgages and credit card bills. The net worth of a company is calculated in the same way—by subtracting liabilities from assets. On a balance sheet, a company's net worth is referred to as shareholders' equity.

Problems arise when a company's balance sheet includes *intangible assets,* such as brand names, that cannot be treated as a normal asset. Most accountants call these strange assets *goodwill,* for lack of a better word. The term rarely refers to any good deeds or charitable efforts on the part of the company. A dot-com company, if it has a well-known portal name, for example, is often worth a lot more than its real assets.

Since intangible assets like goodwill are difficult to evaluate, many analysts prefer to exclude them altogether when calculating the value of old-economy companies such as automobile manufacturers. This figure, called *tangible net worth,* provides a more conservative estimate of the company's value. Obviously, tangible net worth is not of great value in estimating the net worth of a New Economy company such as a Web site. The real assets, such as desks and chairs, make up only a fraction of the company's "real" value.

Net worth is also called *book value* because it shows what would be left on the "books" if the company were to be liquidated—such as after a bankruptcy—and the assets are used to pay off the liabilities. For a New Economy company, where fixed assets are almost nonexistent, there is little chance the creditors would get much. For example, when boo.com, a British online merchant, went bankrupt after going through $300 million in venture capital, for example, the only assets available to creditors were some leftover sporting goods and a lot of barely-used computers.

29. WHAT IS BANKRUPTCY?

THE TERM *BANKRUPTCY* has its origins in medieval Italy, where traders who could not pay their bills had their benches broken *(banca rotta)* to keep them from doing business. Today, a bankrupt company—or individual—has a choice. A bankrupt company may liquidate its assets immediately, or it may be allowed to attempt a recovery, supervised by a legal authority.

Bankruptcy is an integral part of the capitalist system, which uses the lure of profits as the "carrot" to attract investors to a new venture, and the "stick" of bankruptcy to force companies to be run properly. In a socialist or totalitarian system, there is no such thing as bankruptcy. Under capitalism, it is the company's stockholders who share in the glory or pain of both extremes. When a company makes a profit, the shareholders are rewarded in one of two ways: they receive a dividend, or they enjoy the rise in the value of a company's stocks when the profit is added to the balance sheet. When a company loses money, shareholders also lose as dividends are eliminated, or the company's stocks decline in value.

If an ailing company loses so much money that it cannot pay its debts, it declares bankruptcy—which forces its creditors to help find a solution. Basically, shareholders bear most of the pain of bankruptcy as their equity diminishes or disappears altogether, since creditors, including suppliers and bondholders, are paid off first.

In most countries of the world economy, bankrupt companies are encouraged to try to continue operating, under legal supervision, in order to generate money to pay off creditors. Just as a mechanic may try to fix a broken-down car before sending it to the junk heap, companies are sometimes given a new life through court-appointed restructuring. This *rehabilitation* is called Chapter Eleven in the United States—referring to the relevant chapter in the U.S. Bankruptcy Code—and Administration in Britain. Chapter Eleven gives an insolvent company one last opportunity to reorganize and possibly return to profitability.

If a company shows no prospect of being able to recover, it is simply forced into *liquidation*—called Chapter Seven in the United States and Receivership in Britain. Under liquidation, assets are sold off to provide enough funds to pay off at least part of the company's debts. The various terms for bankruptcy used around the world are listed below.

COUNTRY	REHABILITATION	LIQUIDATION
United States	Chapter Eleven	Chapter Seven
Britain, Canada	Administration	Receivership
France	Règlement à l'amiable	Liquidation
Germany	Vergleich	Konkurs
Italy	Amministrazione	Liquidazione
Brazil	Concordata	Falência
Japan	Kaishakoseiho	Tosan

30. WHAT IS VENTURE CAPITAL?

NOTHING VENTURED, NOTHING gained. The old proverb is still appropriate, even in the world of high-tech finance.

Instead of turning to risk-averse banks to borrow money

at potentially high interest rates, many start-up companies, such as dot-coms, turn to private investors who are willing to take a risk and provide "venture" capital. Venture capitalists sometimes pump millions of dollars into the new companies in the hope that, someday, they will profit enormously.

Venture capitalists almost always ask for a share of the company. In order to reward them for taking a risk, they are given stock in return for providing the seed money to get the company up and running. When the company "goes public" and sells its shares on the open market, the venture capital firms that previously invested in it stand to make a big profit.

The problem with most venture capital investments is that they are relatively "illiquid." This means that venture capital investors often have to wait several years before the company is able to show enough profits, or promise of profits, to take the company public—usually accomplished through an Initial Public Offering (IPO), which is arranged by an investment bank, or group of investment banks, called underwriters (see *What Is an IPO?*).

There are many different kinds of venture capitalists. Some are wealthy individuals, sometimes referred to as "angels," who step in to keep a company afloat until it can develop a viable business plan.

Sometimes, companies set up their own venture capital groups. Intel, for example, invested more than two billion dollars in venture investments during the 1990s. These investments were worth more than ten billion dollars by the year 2000. Some private firms create venture capital funds for their own employees, and some accounting firms and law firms have even begun taking pre-IPO companies' shares in lieu of fees.

Traditionally, venture capital firms are small, close-knit partnerships. The partners often spend a lot of time advising and monitoring managers. The idea is to help build the firm slowly, providing technical support in addition to financial support.

Some venture capital firms have set up "incubators," groups that provide the corporate infrastructure small companies need to allow them to turn good ideas into well-run businesses. This support could include anything from providing office space to providing executive recruiters to help the new firms find top managers for selected positions. As the venture capital universe has expanded, partnerships are placing bigger bets on a larger number of companies and therefore have less time to monitor and mentor the start-ups.

Private investors looking to help entrepreneurs "turn their garages into gold" can invest in *venture capital funds*. These funds are often set up by banks or other financial groups to allow small investors to get on the bandwagon. By the end of the 1990s, more than fifty billion dollars was invested in venture capital funds, compared to only three billion at the beginning of the decade.

The basic idea of a venture capital fund is to invest money in a lot of different startup companies, knowing that only a few will probably show a profit. Venture capitalists reckon that those companies, often less than twenty percent, that do succeed, are so profitable that they make up for all the losses on the others. Like Hollywood movies, a lot of start-ups do not pay off, but the ones that do can make a fortune for those who get in at the beginning.

31. WHAT IS AN IPO?

THE ULTIMATE RITE of passage for a young company is to sell its shares to the public through an Initial Public Offering (IPO). When a company "goes public," it usually means allowing its shares to trade on a recognized stock exchange, such as the New York Stock Exchange, the Deutsche Börse in Frankfurt, or the Tokyo Stock Exchange. In the U.S., most Internet-related IPOs trade on the National Association of Securities Dealers Automated Quotation System (NASDAQ).

The major advantage of an IPO is that it provides a growing company with access to a huge investor pool. It also puts a lot of money into the hands of the company's original owners, which may include venture capitalists who invested money in the fledgling company for a share of its stock (see *What Is Venture Capital?*). A publicly traded company also has the advantage of instant credibility with banks, creditors, and customers—and lofty post-IPO stock prices allow a company to use its own shares to finance further expansion or acquire other companies.

Being a publicly quoted company also has its downside. After an IPO, a company has to publish accounting statements quarterly, forcing it to pay attention to demanding investors who often insist on looking at quarterly earnings instead of concentrating on long-term growth. Going public also requires disclosure of all relevant financial information, including the compensation of company officers, so competitors get a free look at the inner workings of the company. And the cost of going public is not unsubstantial: investment banks often keep up to seven percent of the IPO's proceeds.

The path that a company takes to issuing its shares to the public involves several stages. The first is to choose an investment bank, or group of investment banks, to oversee, or "underwrite," the new issue. This process is often referred to as a "bake-off" because investment banks compete with each other, like bakers at a county fair, to tout their skills at pricing and selling the millions of shares to be offered to the public. An IPO's underwriters are also usually responsible for buying up any unsold shares.

In the United States, every IPO has to be registered with the Securities and Exchange Commission (SEC), which requires companies to prepare a "prospectus" providing an in-depth description of the company's activities and all relevant financial figures. The preliminary prospectus is called a "red herring" because of the red lettering across the top of the front page, warning investors that the price of the new shares has not been fixed. Once the prospectus has been approved, it is posted by the SEC on its Web site under the rubric "Edgar Database" (see www.sec.gov).

Once the company is ready to make the plunge, the shares' price is fixed, usually after an extensive "road show" to explain the company to potential investors and gauge market interest. Setting the new shares' price involves a mixture of black magic and market savvy, since there is no sure way of knowing what a company—especially one that has yet to show a profit—is really worth. IPO share prices are often deliberately set low to generate market enthusiasm and ensure that all the shares are placed on the opening day of sale. During the late 1990s, for example, many IPOs saw their share price double or quadruple on the first day of trading, making for a lot of happy investors—especially those who were able to get their shares at the fixed *issue price*.

The first in line to get IPO shares are the so-called *friends and family* that the SEC allows a company to declare as "insiders." The next in line are the big institutional investors and fund managers that form the backbone of the underwriters' client base. The remaining shares are distributed, on a lottery basis, to the individual investors who subscribed for IPO shares. Because it is not uncommon for individuals to receive no IPO shares at all, many investors prefer to buy shares in mutual funds that invest in IPOs or in recently issued IPO stocks.

Companies often prefer an IPO to sell out quickly, which guarantees that later issues of shares, called *secondary offerings,* find a ready and willing investor pool. Usually, investors who made a lot of money on the IPO buy more of the company's shares on the open market or through secondary offerings—even when the share price has gone up considerably. When 3Com spun off "Palm," for example, only about 5 percent of Palm shares were offered to the public through the IPO, which ended up generating enormous unmet demand—3Com shrewdly held back the rest of the shares to sell to the public at a later date.

Once, only a few firms stood a chance of going public. Now, it seems, almost any company can do it: restaurants, celebrities—even many companies that don't have a profit in sight. Many big companies have also used IPOs to "spin off" smaller subsidiaries, such as AT&T's sale of its cellular telephone subsidiary to the public. In several former communist countries—Hungary and Poland, for example—IPOs have been very useful vehicles for putting state-owned companies into the public's hands and putting large amounts of cash into the government's pockets.

Even individuals—including Martha Stewart, Tommy Hilfiger, Dick Clark, and Dr. Everett Koop—have used IPOs to sell shares in their enterprises to the public. Like most IPOs, the price of many of these companies' shares has been extremely volatile, with some rising to spectacular heights only to fall sharply when promised profits failed to materialize.

Several Web pages (such as www.IPO.com, www. IPOMaven.com, and www.IPOhome.com) provide investors with useful IPO information—from extracts of SEC filings to IPO chat groups and bulletin boards, links to CEO interviews, analysis of secondary trading, and news on future IPOs.

32. WHAT IS A LEVERAGED BUYOUT?

BY APPLYING FORCE at the right point—sitting on the edge of a long lever like a playground seesaw, for example—you can lift a large weight with a relatively small amount of strength. Likewise, a *leveraged buyout* (LBO) uses a relatively small investment to buy a large company, usually by borrowing most of the purchase amount from someone else.

The key to any LBO is to use "other people's money" as a lever to purchase a company—and then quickly recover the funds to pay off the loans before the interest payments start hurting. This is usually accomplished by forcing the management to sell off selected assets and "restructure" the firm.

Just as a bank president does not own the bank, a company's managers do not own the company—the shareholders do. And because a company is owned by its shareholders, not its managers, the investors making a leveraged buyout get to call the shots. Anyone who controls a majority of the voting shares can take over a company.

If a company's management decides to oppose the goals of

the new controlling shareholders, it is called a *hostile takeover.* The managers may try to fight back by restructuring the company or selling off assets, which makes the company unattractive for the "takeover artists." Other *poison pill* defenses may include buying back the company's shares in the open market, which drives up the price of shares, making a takeover prohibitively expensive.

Sometimes managers may decide to get into the LBO game themselves, deciding that "if you can't beat 'em, join 'em." In a *management buyout,* the managers arrange to take over the company themselves, often borrowing enormous amounts of money to buy a controlling number of shares.

International leveraged buyouts can sometimes be prohibited by governments. This is often the case in countries with *dirigiste* tendencies, such as France, where the "national good" is seen as more important than any individual stockholder's rights. In the United States, the government decided, for reasons of "national security," that airlines could not be majority-owned by foreigners.

Normally, LBO specialists buy undervalued companies that own a large amount of underperforming assets such as cash, real estate, or other holdings. By breaking up the company and selling off valuable assets in a process called *asset stripping,* the mountain of debt used to acquire the company can be paid off. Many successful LBOs are financed by *junk bonds,* high-yielding securities that attract investors by offering extremely high interest rates.

When a leveraged buyout works well, the shareholders—and the economy—are better off. The company often becomes more efficient and more valuable for the new shareholders. If it does not work—if the debt load becomes unbearable, for example, and the company is forced to declare bankruptcy—jobs are destroyed and the original investors lose a lot of money. As with everything else in the world economy, there is no such thing as a sure bet.

33. WHAT IS A MULTINATIONAL?

ANY COMPANY THAT operates outside its home country is a multinational. In the digital age, many companies—from online booksellers in Seattle to porn Web sites in Copenhagen—have become international in scope. The Internet and the gradual removal of trade barriers around the world have made it possible for almost any company to become a multinational with the click of a mouse.

Many multinational companies have adapted the environmental movements' "Think Globally, Act Locally" slogan, as they find that it is no longer appropriate to apply a one-world strategy to international business. And as they do more business around the world, companies have to increasingly respond to cultural and economic differences. For this reason, multinationals as diverse as Coca-Cola and DaimlerChrysler have decentralized decision-making to adapt better to local markets. Many multinationals' corporate headquarters merely coordinate the locally managed activities of their operations abroad.

At IBM, for example, each foreign subsidiary has its own culture and its own local way of doing things. The U.S. headquarters has been progressively reduced, or downsized, to serve as a central clearing house to which hundreds of foreign and domestic profit centers report their results. Management of each of these profit centers is increasingly left to the local managers.

In this way, a Japanese client of IBM sees the Tokyo office as essentially a Japanese company, while a German client perceives the Frankfurt IBM office to be essentially German. This scenario is repeated around the globe: From Buenos Aires to Bombay, IBM has "devoluted" the decision-making power to locally managed offices. The same process is being used by almost every multinational company around the world.

Mercedes Benz vehicles are now produced in Alabama, but its stock is quoted as DaimlerChrysler in Frankfurt and New York. Nestlé is perceived to be a "local" company in many countries around the world, even though its headquarters are in Switzerland. *Reader's Digest* and *Playboy* have launched local editions around the world. Ford, almost from the beginning, has been a global company, producing cars in such faraway locations as Argentina and Australia as early as the 1920s.

The enormous size of multinational companies has led alternately to praise and scorn over the past years. In the 1970s multinationals were often denounced as monopolistic monsters intent on taking over the world. In the 1980s and '90s, they gradually came to be seen as vehicles of change, bringing new capital, new ideas, and above all new jobs to the world economy. At the dawn of the twenty-first century, multinationals are back in the news, as protesters from Seattle to Moscow once again denounce them as forces of evil in the world, destroying the environment and exploiting workers.

In many developing countries, multinational companies provide thousands of new jobs yearly—albeit at salaries that are significantly lower than in the multinationals' home countries. Before criticizing this discrepancy, however, it is important to look at what a salary can actually buy in the country where it is earned. It might seem unfair that a worker in Turkey earns only half of what a worker in Germany earns for doing the same job, but the fact is that a worker in Ankara can live on far less than a worker in Berlin.

Several human-rights groups, including the Fair Labor Association, the United Nations, and the Organization for Economic Cooperation and Development (see *What Role Do Charities and NGOs Play in the World Economy?*), have built various coalitions of consumers, activists, governments, and business leaders to monitor multinationals and work with them to ensure that workers' rights are respected and the environment is preserved—both at home and abroad.

34. WHAT ARE THE RISKS OF INTERNATIONAL INVESTING?

10-YEAR RETURN ON VARIOUS INTERNATIONAL INVESTMENTS

(What $10,000 invested in 1990 would have become by the year 2000)

High-Tech U.S. Stocks (NASDAQ)	$79,471
Blue Chip U.S. Stocks (Dow Jones Industrial Average)	$53,926
Broadly-based U.S. Stock Portfolio (S&P 500 Index)	$53,078
Broadly-based European Stock Portfolio	$36,530
Small Company U.S. Stocks (Russell 2000 Stock Index)	$35,167
International Stocks (Morgan Stanley Capital International)	$21,076
Long-Term U.S. Government Bonds	$19,532
U.S. Money Market Fund	$17,530
Pork Bellies	$16,806
U.S. Property	$14,802
Crude Oil	$13,488
U.S. Inflation (Consumer Price Index)	$13,250

Put under a mattress	$10,000
Platinum	$8,765
Japanese Stocks	$8,606
Art (Paintings)	$6,800
Gold	$6,512

Sources: Piper Jaffrey, UBS AG, *The Economist,* Morgan Stanley Capital International.

Comparing international investments is a difficult business. How can you compare an investment in Japanese stocks to an investment in silver bullion? How can the purchase of a vacation house in Mexico be compared to the purchase of a mutual fund or a U.S. Treasury bond?

Just as different fruits can be compared by weight, international investments have to be evaluated by looking at their total return—or *yield.* This includes the total increase in value, including dividends and other payments, as well as the gains or losses from converting the investment from one currency to another.

College endowment funds, insurance companies, individual investors—whoever is investing abroad—have to decide on one currency of reference and translate all investments into that currency if they want to compare them. A U.S. college endowment fund, which invests billions of dollars abroad, would first translate all those investments into dollars to see how they stack up against each other. In this way, the return on any investment—from stocks and commodities to art and real estate—can be easily evaluated.

Yield is usually defined as the percentage increase in value over a given period of time. But yield is only one factor to consider in evaluating international investments. A prudent investor has to consider a wide range of variables when contemplating any foray into the world of global finance. Investors in the emerging markets of Southeast Asia, for example, saw the value of their investments flourish during the 1990s as the booming economies racked up double-digit gains for most of the decade. When the Asian Crisis hit, however, many ventures were pushed to the brink of bankruptcy and investors bailed out with huge losses. Those who had the courage to stay in saw their fortunes improve when countries such as South Korea and Thailand recovered after painful economic and political reform.

Although international investing often carries high risks, it also provides high rewards. Global investors—from first-time individual investors to experienced pension fund professionals—need to look carefully at each country's political and economic situation before sending their money abroad. By identifying, and sometimes removing, the risks involved, the wheel of fortune of the global markets can spin in the investor's favor. Banks, for example, have made a science of weighing the various risks in international investing. When lending money to foreign borrowers, they not only consider the traditional "domestic" risks of credit, maturity, interest rates and so forth, but they identify additional hazards, such as *exchange risk* and *political risk*.

Exchange risk—changes in the value of foreign currencies—can sometimes work in the investor's favor, providing additional profits if the foreign currency gains in value. On the other hand, if the foreign currency plummets, the loss could wipe out the earnings from an otherwise lucrative international investment. A California employees' fund that invests in Tokyo, for example, may see the value of the stocks and bonds go up as the Japanese market booms, but if the yen loses value against the U.S. dollar, those foreign "earnings" may end up being a loss in U.S. dollar terms. On the other hand, a foreign investor in Japanese stocks would gain doubly if the yen increased in value.

Political risk is also an important component of any international investment. If the government is overthrown or if new laws are passed restricting the transfer of funds abroad—both occurred during the Asian Crisis—foreign investors sometimes lose everything. Even countries that are not part of the trouble spot are affected, as foreign investment money flees for safer harbors.

Rating agencies, such as Moody's and Standard & Poor's, can help global investors evaluate risk (see *How Are Ratings Used to Evaluate International Investments?*). Essentially, countries can be rated just like companies, with "investment grade" reserved for only those countries with stable governments and open borders to trade and investment. In the end, after all the risks have been calculated, international investment can provide a high return that rewards the investor for the various risks taken.

35. WHAT IS A STOCK INDEX?

IT IS NOT necessary for a farmer to examine every plant in the field to see how a crop is growing. It is usually sufficient to look at a few plants in various parts of the field to get a good idea of the progress of the crop as a whole.

Likewise, an investor does not have to look at every stock traded to see where the market moved on a particular day. It is sufficient to look at the prices of a small group of stocks, making up an *index,* which is used to represent the stock market as a whole.

Every stock market around the world has at least one

index that tracks the movements of a group of representative stocks. The Dow Jones Industrial Average, for example, tracks the prices of thirty of the most prestigious "blue-chip" stocks, mainly from the New York Stock Exchange (NYSE) but now including stocks from the technology-laden NASDAQ exchange as well. Sometimes, it is more useful to look at a "broad" index that takes the weighted average of hundreds of shares, such as the Standard & Poor's (S&P) index, which measures the movement of five hundred different stocks from several different exchanges.

The prices of the shares in each group of stocks are usually *indexed,* which means that more weight is given to the price changes of stock for large companies. When IBM or Nippon Telephone & Telegraph move sharply, they are given more weight in the S&P index than the price movements of smaller companies. There are exceptions, such as the Dow Jones Indexes in Tokyo and New York, which simply average the prices of every stock in the group, regardless of its relative importance to the market.

In some countries, a major bank might calculate the main stock index, while in others, the stock exchanges—such as the NASDAQ or the Swiss Performance Index—provide their own compilation. In some markets, a news agency, such as Dow Jones, provides investors with an index that measures the market's activities on any particular day. In Japan, the Nikkei Index receives its name from the acronym of Japan's leading financial newspaper, the *Nihon Keizai Shimbun.* In London, the *Financial Times* provides the most widely watched stock index, the FTSE, commonly referred to as the "footsie."

Cross-border stock indexes are difficult to calculate because they often contain stocks denominated in different currencies. The EURO STOXX index overcomes this by only looking at stocks traded in euro-area countries. A wider European index, the STOXX, includes stocks from non-euro countries such as Switzerland and England, so its movement reflects currency changes as well as changes in the price of stocks. Technology stock indexes include the Pacific Exchange Tech Index and the S&P Tech Composite Index in North America. Germany's *Neuer Markt* and France's *Nouveau Marché* also provide specialized indices for continental Europe's New Economy stocks. In Japan, the major tech index is the Topix Electric Index.

Wherever the market, someone is watching—and this information is provided in the form of stock indexes to investors from around the world.

INTERNATIONAL STOCK MARKET INDEXES AND AVERAGES

Argentina, Buenos Aires: Merval Index (Mercado de Valores),
    www.bcba.sba.com.ar
Australia, Sydney: All Ordinaries Index, www.asx.com.au
Austria, Vienna: ATX Index (Austrian Traded Index), www.wbag.at
Belgium, Brussels: BEL-20 Index, www.stockexchange.be
Brazil, São Paulo: Bovespa Index, www.bovespa.com.br
Britain, London: FT-SE 100 (Financial Times Stock Exchange Index),
    www.stockex.co.uk
Canada, Toronto: TSE Industrials (Toronto Stock Exchange), www.tse.com
Chile, Santiago: IGPA Index, www.bolsantiago.cl
China, Shenzhen, Shanghai: B Shares Index, www.chinaweb.com
Czech Republic, Prague: PX 50 Index, www.pse.cz
Denmark, Copenhagen: Stock Index, www.xcse.dk
Finland, Helsinki: HEX General Index (Helsinki Stock Exchange), www.hex.fi
France, Paris: CAC-40 Index, www.bourse-de-paris.fr
Germany, Frankfurt: DAX (Deutscher Aktien-Index), www.exchange.de
Greece, Athens: Composite Index, www.ase.gr
Hong Kong: Hang Seng Index, www.sehk.com.hk
Hungary, Budapest: Bux Index (Budapest Stock Exchange), www.bse.hu
India, Bombay: Sensex 30 (Bombay Stock Exchange Sensitive Index),
    www.bseindia.com
Indonesia, Jakarta: Composite Index, www.jsx.co.id
Israel, Tel Aviv: Tel Aviv 25 Index, www.tase.co.il

Italy, Milan: MIB Telematico (Milano Indice di Borsa), www.borsaitalia.it

Japan, Tokyo: Nikkei 225, www.tse.or.jp

Korea, Seoul: Composite Index, www.kse.or.kr

Malaysia, Kuala Lumpur: Composite Index, www.klse.com.my

Mexico, Mexico City: Bolsa Index, www.bmv.com.mx

Netherlands, Amsterdam: AEX Index (Amsterdam Stock Exchange), www.aex.nl

New Zealand, Wellington: NZSE-40 Index, www.nzse.co.nz

Nigeria, Lagos: SE All-Share Index, www.nse.com.ng

Norway, Oslo: OBX Industrial Index (Oslo Bourse Index), www.ose.no

Pakistan, Karachi: KSE (Karachi Stock Exchange) Index, www.kse.com.pk

Philippines, Manila: PSE Index (Philippines Stock Exchange), www.pse.org.ph

Russia, Moscow: Moscow Times Index, www.moscowtimes.ru/markets

Singapore: Straits Times Index, www.ses.com.sg

South Africa, Johannesburg: All Market Index, www.jse.co.za

Spain, Madrid: Bolsa Index, www.bolsamadrid.es

South Korea, Seoul: Composite Index, www.kse.or.kr

Sweden, Stockholm: SX Index, www.omgroup.com

Switzerland, Zürich: SPI Index (Swiss Performance Index), www.bourse.ch

Taiwan, Taipei: Stock Market Index, www.tse.com.tw

Thailand, Bangkok: SET Index (Stock Exchange of Thailand), www.set.or.th

Turkey, Istanbul: National 100 Index, www.ise.org

United States, New York:

    New York Stock Exchange, www.nyse.com

    Dow Jones Industrial Average, www.dowjones.com

    Standard & Poor 500, www.spglobal.com

    NASDAQ (National Association of Securities Dealers Automated Quotation System), www.nasdaq.com

Venezuela, Caracas: IBC Index, www.caracasstock.com

Warsaw, Poland: WIG-20 Index, www.gpw.com.pl

Regional/Global Indexes:

    DJ Stoxx 50, Pan European Stocks, www.stoxx.com

    DJ Euro Stoxx 50 (stocks from countries using the Euro), www.stoxx.com

    MSCI (Morgan Stanley Capital International World Index), www.msci.com

    World Bond Market: J.P. Morgan Government Bond Index, www.jpmorgan.com

        S&P Emerging-Market Investable Index, www.spglobal.com

36. HOW DO INVESTORS BUY
FOREIGN SHARES?

ONLINE TRADING NOW makes it possible to buy almost any stock in the world, twenty-four hours a day. Web-based brokers such as the E*Trade Group allow Swedish investors to buy U.S. stocks online and pay for the investments in Swedish krones. Online traders now allow clients to buy shares in any country in the world, in almost any currency they choose.

As foreign markets expand their role in the world economy, investors have begun to expand their portfolios as well. Someone in one part of the world can go on the Web and buy shares in foreign markets with little more effort than it takes to buy shares at home.

One way to buy foreign shares is to use a broker—online or the old-fashioned way, via the telephone. In this way, an investor can buy Club Med shares in France or Toyota shares in Tokyo, and then have the shares deposited in a local brokerage account. In most cases, however, the foreign share's price will still be quoted in the foreign currency, and the dividends, if there are any, will not be in the investor's home currency either.

To avoid these inconveniences, many companies have their shares listed as *stock certificates* on various exchanges around the world. In North America, these are called American Depositary Receipts. ADRs are created by banks that buy shares of a foreign company and place them on deposit in the United States.

These foreign stock certificates give the holder the rights to the *underlying share*. When the foreign share changes its value, the stock certificate changes its value as well. In this way, the buyer of an ADR for Toyota does not have to keep track of the yen price of the share. The ADR price is quoted in U.S. dollars on North American exchanges and the dividends are credited— again, in dollars—to the owner's normal brokerage account.

Some foreign shares are listed directly on various exchanges around the world. The New York Stock Exchange, for example, trades the shares of several hundred foreign companies. This provides investors with liquid, easy-to-trade stocks that have been approved by the Securities and Exchange Commission, as well as financial figures according to U.S. norms. If the stock is quoted in dollars in New York, its value is still affected by the currency exchange rate. If the yen goes up against the dollar, the holder of a Toyota ADR will benefit, even if the stock price has not changed a bit in Tokyo.

Besides traditional *registered shares,* some countries, such as Switzerland, offer investors the choice of *bearer shares,* which do not require the registration of the owner's name at the company's headquarters. Other international investment vehicles—available in several countries around the world—include *participation certificates,* which provide dividends like normal shares but do not allow the investor to vote at stockholders' meetings.

In some developing countries, foreign ownership of shares is still prohibited or made extremely difficult. It is therefore sometimes easier for investors to buy shares in a *country fund,* which consists of local shares put into funds that are made available to investors from other parts of the world.

Despite the ease of trading provided by all these new international exchanges, cross-border investing is still not seamless. National accounting laws require companies to adhere to strict local accounting rules, and some companies do not make the effort to adapt their financial statements to make them comprehensible to foreign investors. Many global companies, however, prepare different sets of books for various markets around the world. Investors can also learn about foreign companies just by clicking a mouse: CNN, Bloomberg, and many other news sources provide online reports for almost every publicly quoted company in the world.

37. WHAT IS AN EQUITY FUND?

INSTEAD OF PUTTING all of their eggs in one basket, international investors often buy funds that hold several different shares, thereby spreading the risks of investing over a wide range of companies. Essentially, equity funds allow investors to avoid the pain of losing all of their money on one bankrupt company.

Equity funds normally use professional fund managers to choose which securities—stocks and stock options, mostly—to put in the fund. In theory, these professionals understand individual markets better than the average investor and are consequently better able to avoid making costly mistakes.

A plethora of equity funds are available for the international investor. *Growth stock funds* invest primarily in companies that retain their earnings and concentrate on rapid growth. *Income stock funds* hold shares in well-established companies that pay consistent dividends. This may be of interest for a pension fund, or for retired people who need a constant "fixed" income. *Country funds* and *regional funds* provide investors with an opportunity to share in the growth of special foreign markets.

Technology funds (see *What Is Venture Capital?*) offer the possibility for huge future gains—with little expectation of the company providing any income in the first few years. The fact that technological change occurs in different parts of the world at different times allows smart investors to anticipate new "waves" of growth before they happen. In Europe, for example, Internet companies only began to take off after the dot-com wave had already peaked in the United States.

Essentially, there are two types of structures for equity funds. A "closed end" fund (called an "investment trust" in Britain) has a limited number of shares available. These shares are traded on the open markets, where their price is determined by supply and demand. The fund's shares may go down in value, but the shares in the fund could rise if there are not enough to meet demand. In an "open end" fund (called a "unit trust" in Britain), new shares can be issued at any time. The price is determined not by supply and demand, but by the underlying value of the fund's holdings, sometimes referred to as Net Asset Value (NAV).

Politically or socially conscious investors, such as college endowment funds, can invest in equity funds that correspond to their view of how the world should be run. A socially conscious fund may invest only in companies that guarantee non-discrimination for race, sex, or sexual orientation. While others may guarantee that the companies they invest in do not destroy the environment—by planting a tree, for example, for every one that is harvested. Although it is hard to choose any one company that is one hundred percent in tune with investors' social or environmental goals, these various equity funds often choose to list the best companies in their group—selecting natural resources companies, for example, that do the *least* amount of damage to the environment.

Investors can also invest in groups of companies that are

listed on socially conscious and environmentally conscious indexes. Some examples are: the Domini 400 Social Index in the United States, the Jantzi Social Index in Canada, the NPI Social Index in Britain, as well as the Dow Jones Sustainability Group of international stocks.

38. WHAT IS A CAPITAL MARKET?

CAPITAL, OR ACCUMULATED WEALTH, forms the basis for all economic activity in market-oriented, or *capitalist,* societies. Capital is money, and it is represented by *securities*—bonds mostly—that are traded on the world's capital markets just like any other commodity.

The price borrowers pay for money is the interest rate. This "price" is determined by supply and demand. When there is a shortage of money to lend, borrowers have to pay a higher interest rate. When money is plentiful, interest rates decline.

There is no single center for capital market trading. The world's securities are traded in a vast network of electronically linked banks and securities houses located all over the world—from Tokyo and Singapore to London and New York. The international capital markets serve one major purpose: to get money from those who have it into the hands of those who want it and are willing to pay a price to get it. Hundreds of billions of dollars—and euros, and yen, and pounds—are traded daily on the world's capital markets.

The international capital markets bring together a wide variety of borrowers and lenders. Investors can be as large as the

California State Employees' Retirement Fund or as small as a Swiss farmer buying a bond at a local bank. Borrowers include corporations, governments, and international organizations— from IBM to the Kingdom of Sweden to the African Development Bank.

How does it work? When a Swiss investor buys a bond of the African Development Bank, the primary motivation isn't necessarily to give money to Africa, even though that is the final result. An investor is looking for a "return" on the investment. Borrowers on the world's capital markets have to assure investors that the bond will be paid back on time along with all the interest payments. Development banks such as the World Bank or the African Development Bank have the implicit backing of rich-country governments, so investors are willing to loan development banks money at relatively low interest rates (see *What Are Regional Development Banks?*).

Basically, capital markets facilitate the transfer of money from one part of the world to another, where it can be used for development and growth. The Swiss farmer doesn't need it right away, and the African farmer's cooperative, which may need to build a new well, does.

39. WHAT IS A BOND?

UNLIKE A STOCK, which represents the risk and reward of ownership in a company, a bond is simply a loan agreement that says: "I, the borrower, agree to pay to you, the bondholder, a certain amount of money at a certain time in the future."

Anyone can issue a bond, so long as someone is willing to buy it. The buyer of the bond is essentially lending money to the issuer and has reasonable confidence that the bond will be paid back at some time in the future, along with the agreed amount of interest.

A bond is basically an IOU, a piece of paper giving the *bondholder* the right to two things. First the bond's *issuer,* the borrower, has to pay back the *principal,* the original amount borrowed. Second, the issuer has to pay interest periodically, to reward those who have bought the bond as an investment. These interest payments are often called *coupons.* This term refers to the little pieces of paper that were attached to the bonds before electronic markets made paper transactions unnecessary.

When an investor decides to sell a bond before its final maturity, it is necessary to determine its value. A $1000 bond paying 8 percent interest annually is certainly worth more than one issued by the same borrower that only pays 5 percent, but how much more?

It is first necessary to calculate how much interest is going to be paid over the bond's life. This *return* is then compared with other bonds and interest-bearing investments in the market-place. Bond prices are constantly raised or lowered to reflect this comparative analysis.

Essentially, bond prices are determined by interest rates. A bond paying a relatively low rate of interest is sold at a *discount,* a lower price, when bonds with higher interest rates are issued by the same type of borrower. A low-coupon bond issued by Intel, for example, may have to be sold for 90 percent of its *face value,* or redemption value, to make it attractive enough to compete with a new bond issued by the same company with higher interest rates. By paying less for a bond, the buyer receives a higher return, called *yield.*

Like a playground seesaw, when one side—the bond's

price—goes down, the other side—the bond's yield—goes up. When interest rates fall, the price of existing bonds rise. In a period of declining interest rates, a relatively high-coupon bond would see its price increase until its yield is the same as other bonds in the market with similar maturity and similar risk. A bond's price may easily rise above its face value—to 110 percent, for example—to make its yield comparable with other bonds in the market.

Bond yields and bond prices are also determined by the bond's risk—the likelihood of being repaid. The riskier the borrower, the more a potential investor will have to be paid. A Brazilian sugar company with a high risk of going bankrupt would pay higher interest on its bonds than the Kingdom of Sweden. Bonds, especially government bonds, are seen as relatively safe investments. The amount of bonds that *default,* or go unpaid, is quite small.

In the international capital markets, the U.S. Treasury bond serves as an indicator of the market as a whole. Since there is virtually no risk that the U.S. government would ever default on a dollar-denominated bond—basically, all it would have to do is print up more dollars to pay off the bondholders—U.S. Treasury bonds are used as a *benchmark.* All other dollar-denominated bonds trade at a *spread,* or difference in yield, to the U.S. Treasury bonds. Other government securities, such as the British *gilt* and German *bunds,* are also seen as benchmarks in their own markets because they have the explicit backing of the governments that issue them.

40. WHAT ARE EUROCURRENCIES AND EUROBONDS?

DURING THE COLD War, the Soviet Union was—understandably—reluctant to put its U.S. dollar reserves under the control of authorities in the United States. So, instead of putting its dollars on deposit in New York, it turned to European banks to keep those dollars abroad. Those deposits were soon being called *Eurodollars* to differentiate them from dollars kept on deposit in their home country.

Today, any currency held abroad, even in banks that are not in Europe, is called a *Eurocurrency*. Japanese yen held in a New York bank, for example, are called Euroyen. Even the new European currency, the euro, can be held abroad. Euros held in Japan would be called—appropriately enough—"Euro-euros."

By the 1980s and 1990s, a huge market had developed for Eurocurrencies, mainly centered in London. Arab oil producers, following the example of the Soviet Union, began keeping a large part of their "petrodollars" in European banks. This flood of foreign capital needed to be invested, so London-based banks began issuing U.S. dollar bonds, outside the control and regulations of the U.S. government. These bonds were called *Eurobonds*. Soon, the world's banks and securities houses were all issuing Eurobonds in all of the major currencies.

Investors liked the fact that Eurobonds were *bearer bonds*. Unlike normal domestic bonds, which were registered with the government, bearer bonds allow the investor to remain anonymous. And since there was no withholding tax on interest payments, investors could pocket the interest income without reporting it to the tax authorities at home.

When American corporations found out they could issue bonds more cheaply abroad, with lower interest rates and fewer restrictions than in the United States, the London-based Eurobond market grew even more, quickly outstripping most of the world's other financial centers. Only by reducing restrictions on new issues of securities in the United States was the U.S. government able to return international capital market activity—in U.S. dollars, at least—to American shores.

41. HOW ARE RATINGS USED TO EVALUATE INTERNATIONAL INVESTMENTS?

EXAMINING FINANCIAL DOCUMENTS from companies around the world would be a daunting task for any investor, no matter how knowledgeable. Most investors, therefore, have come to rely on ratings agencies to help them judge the risk of countries abroad and the companies that do business in them.

The first question an investor asks, especially when buying bonds or other fixed-rate securities, is: "What are the chances of getting my money back?" A bond investor not only needs to know whether the interest on the "loan" will be paid back (see *What Is a Bond?*), but also whether the principal, or the amount of money originally invested, will be repaid.

An important thing to remember when investing abroad is to always look at the country rating first. A sovereign government is usually a better credit risk than a company in that country. The government, in theory, will always be the last to go bankrupt. If a company has assets to pay its loans, it is assumed the government could seize those assets in order to pay off its debts first. Of course, with multinational companies—and more and more companies have assets in countries other the one in which they are domiciled—all bets are off.

The best way to judge a company's or a country's risk is to look at its rating. The world's two largest ratings agencies, Moody's Investors Services and Standard & Poor's (S&P), both provide a "Triple A" rating for the healthiest countries and companies. For example, loans to "AAA" borrowers, such as the United States and Switzerland, are considered to offer the best chance of being paid back on time—with interest, of course. Duff & Phelps, another ratings agency, also uses the AAA system, while A.M. Best uses grade-school style letters like A++ to denote the best borrowers.

	MOODY'S	S&P	DUFF & PHELPS
	www.moodysratings.com	**www.S&P.com**	**www.dcrco.com**
Investment Grade	Aaa	AAA	AAA
	Aa	AA	AA
	A	A	A
	Baa	BBB	BBB
Speculative	Ba	BB	BB
	B	B	B
Very Risky	Caa,Ca,C	CCC,CC	CCC,CC,C

Since many large pension and money-management funds are required to hold only "investment-grade" securities, when a country is upgraded, as Mexico was in 2000, the country's leaders and company's owners rejoice. Not only does a higher rating mean a lower "cost of capital," in that the government can issue bonds with lower interest rates, the companies in a higher-rated country usually see their own ratings improve, and they are able to get access to cheaper funding as well. A dot-com startup in Mexico, for example, becomes much more profitable—and competitive—when it is able to borrow money at rates similar to those in Silicon Valley.

42. HOW IS GOLD PART OF THE WORLD ECONOMY?

GOLD CAN BE bought and sold in almost every market and currency imaginable, whether in a Cairo *souk* or a sophisticated commodity exchange in Chicago.

Although some gold trading is based on commercial transactions, such as an Amsterdam jeweler buying gold for inventory, most gold is purchased as an investment. Gold investors range from powerful central banks that use gold to shore up their currencies to individuals who hope gold will be the one thing to hold its value in inflationary times.

Gold's role in the world economy has been changing. Before banks and security houses became part of the electronically connected "global village," gold served as a uniquely liquid investment that could be exchanged anywhere in the world at any given time. People in war-torn countries still use gold as a refuge. Many of the refugees fleeing the war in Kosovo, for example, used small amounts of gold or gold jewelry to buy their way to safety.

In developed economies, gold is perceived mostly as a "hedge"—it provides a stable refuge for investors if world markets should crash or if inflation should rear up its ugly head.

When inflation is brought under control, however, gold loses its luster: unlike most other investments, there is no interest paid on gold. The only possible hope for profit is for gold to rise in value on the world markets, giving the investors a capital gain. Central banks have been the world's biggest gold holders, but as inflation worries receded during the late 1990s, they began selling off some of their large holdings in order to put the money to better use.

There are several ways of investing in gold, including buying shares in gold mining companies or gold mutual funds. Most gold investments are "spot" purchases for immediate delivery. Gold is usually held in a custodian bank that charges a fee for storage—a form of "negative interest rate."

Gold trading takes place in banks and trading houses all over the world as well as on the Web. One favorite method of buying gold is to purchase a *future*. Purchases that are not for immediate delivery are called futures contracts, because they are based on specific delivery dates in the future, usually occurring every three months. Tailor-made futures contracts, with flexible dates to fit the needs of specific buyers and sellers, are called forward contracts. Gold futures prices, like a child riding piggyback, tend to move in the same direction as gold spot prices. Also, they often rise and fall in tandem with the prices of other precious metals, such as silver and platinum.

43. WHAT ARE DERIVATIVES?

IT MAY SOUND like a house of cards, but many financial instruments in the global economy are based on nothing more than the value of other financial instruments. This scares many investors, and derivatives are often blamed for many of the excesses in the world economy. In fact, derivatives are not necessarily any riskier than any other investment in the global marketplace—they just have to be properly understood.

A derivative, as its name implies, "derives" its value from another item of value. A financial future, for example, is an agreement to buy a financial instrument, such as a stock or a bond, at some point in the future. If the stock price then goes up—or if interest rates move dramatically, affecting the price of the underlying bonds—a financial future can skyrocket or plummet precipitously.

Many investors, primarily those looking for a quick profit without carefully analyzing the risks involved, have been burned by the explosion of derivative trading on the international markets. California's Orange County, for example, became insolvent during the 1990s after investing heavily in interest-rate-linked derivatives.

What makes derivatives risky is not the instrument itself; it's the speed with which it can rise or fall. When markets change direction quickly, with interest rates falling or rising rapidly, for example, investors in derivatives can see their portfolios rise or fall precipitously.

Some derivatives can actually allow investors to avoid risk, giving them the possibility to "hedge" otherwise risky positions (see glossary entries for *Stock Index Futures, Swaps, Program Trading,* and *Warrants*). A retired homeowner, for example, may use an investment in interest-rate derivatives to counterbalance the effect of inflation on the value of the home.

The most commonly used derivatives in the world economy are call and put options (see *What Are Stock Options?* and *What Is a Currency Option?*).

44. WHAT IS AN OPTION?

IT IS ALWAYS worthwhile to keep your options open. That trustworthy advice applies to the world of international finance as well. There is always value in having the right, but not the obligation, to buy or sell something at a guaranteed price in the future.

A racehorse owner with an option to buy a new thoroughbred at a certain price could exercise that option with great profit if the horse were to win the Kentucky Derby. A sheep farmer in New Zealand could profit from having the option to sell wool at a guaranteed price at the end of each season if the price of wool were to fall precipitously.

In the financial markets, where nothing of value is free, options—logically—cost money. The seller of the option has to be paid for taking the risk that the option will be exercised, or used at some time in the future.

One of the biggest advantages of buying an option is that investors know they will never lose more than the price they originally paid for the option. If wool prices in New Zealand end up higher than the level guaranteed by the purchase option the New Zealand farmer can choose to let the call option expire and sell wool on the open market at the higher price.

The most important factor in determining an option's value is the likelihood of it being used. An option that no one expects to be exercised costs very little. However, an option will naturally be quite expensive if there is a good chance of its being exercised. An option to buy a ton of umbrellas would be more expensive just before a London rainstorm than during a dry spell in Los Angeles.

Options can be created for anything that has uncertainty. For example, since no one knows for sure if a stock's price will go up or down, it is worthwhile having an option to sell a given stock at a fixed price in the future. If its price moves in the right direction, the holder of a stock option will profit handsomely by exercising that option—or by selling it to someone else.

An option's value essentially depends on the movement in value of the underlying asset. But two other factors also influence an option's value: *volatility,* the amount of movement of the underlying asset's price; and *time value,* the amount of time for which the option is valid. An option based on a high-volatility asset, such as a dot-com stock, is worth much more than one based on a stock that hardly ever changes in value. Likewise, an option that can be exercised over several years is much more valuable than one that can be exercised for only a few days.

Because options are much more volatile than the underlying assets on which they are based, investors need to be especially careful with them. Buying an option is not the same as buying a stock. It can rise exponentially in value, or it can become worthless within a matter of weeks. Because a stock option, for example, represents the right to buy or sell a large number of shares of the underlying stock, its price moves much more quickly—in both directions—than the stock price itself (see *What Are Stock Options?*).

The world's first options were used in early agrarian societies, where options in the form of handshake agreements allowed farmers to hedge against the fluctuating price of commodities such as wheat or grapes. In the expanding global economy, options and option markets—from Chicago to Hong Kong, from Melbourne to London—have grown to include a vast cornucopia of products, including foreign currency options and options on other financial instruments such as stock indexes, futures, and interest rates.

45. WHAT ARE STOCK OPTIONS?

WHEN A HIGH-tech startup company offers to pay its employees in stock options—bringing dreams of becoming a billionaire overnight—the instrument they are referring to is a *call option*. Stock options are, by far, the most popular form of options in the world economy. They give the right to buy or sell a certain number of shares, called *underlying shares,* at a certain price in the future.

Call options give the right to the holder to buy, or "call in," something at a certain price and at a certain time in the future. *Put options* give the holder the right to sell, or "put" something into the option seller's hands, at a certain price and at a certain time in the future. A smart career move, at least in a volatile Silicon Valley company, would probably be to ask for both call *and* put options before signing any contract.

A stock option, like any call option, is manna from heaven for investors who think the company's shares are going to go up. Having the right—but not the obligation—to buy a company's shares for a certain price in the future allows investors to profit when the stock's price goes up. If the share's price goes high enough, the holder of a call option would exercise the right to buy the shares at a price lower than the market price. These newly purchased shares could then be resold on the market for a profit. Alternatively, the holder of a call option can sell the option to someone else and pocket the profit—thereby avoiding the trouble of buying and selling shares on the open market.

Who would buy a put option? Investors who think the markets are going to take a fall. Owning a put on a stock gives the investor the right to sell the company's shares at a fixed price. If the shares' price were to drop below the *striking price* of the option, the investor gains. Either the investor buys shares on the open market and uses the put option to sell them at a higher price, or, more commonly, the investor simply sells the valuable put option to someone else.

Basically, call and put options give the investor a lot more "bang for their buck." Instead of using a lot of capital to buy the underlying assets, option investors can, for a relatively small amount of money invested, profit handsomely if the market moves in the right direction.

Who issues options? Whoever wants to take a risk in the opposite direction. The key is to have the financial wherewithal, however, to back up the promise made by each option. Many high-tech companies, for example, have issued enormous amounts of employee stock options over the past years.

What happens when employees begin exercising their stock options? The company has two choices. It can go out into the market and buy enough stocks to sell to its employees at cut-rate prices, or it can issue new shares, which has the effect of diluting the value of other shares held by investors. In the year 2000, for example, Dell Computer had to spend several billion dollars buying back shares in the market—wiping out nearly its entire net income for that period—when employees decided to exercise their numerous stock options.

Because the world markets for options and other derivatives have become so complex, investors (particularly those managing other people's money) need to carefully weigh all of the risks involved before they venture into the exciting—and volatile—world of options trading.

46. WHAT IS A CURRENCY OPTION?

ANYONE PLANNING A business venture in another country would like to know what the foreign currency is going to be worth when the time comes to change money. Unwelcome currency fluctuations could make a shipment of wine from Chili or a BMW import from Germany prohibitively expensive when it arrives.

Currency options allow individual investors, businesses, or merchants to lock in the future value of a foreign currency. By buying or selling a currency option, it is possible to fix exactly how many Swiss francs or Japanese yen a U.S. dollar can buy at any given time in the future. Just like other options, a currency option gives the holder the right, but not the obligation, to buy or sell something at a fixed price—in this case, a currency. The most common currency options are based on the U.S. dollar price of Swiss francs, euros, British pounds, and Japanese yen.

Like all investments in the international marketplace, currency options can be used for speculation. Investors who believe that a currency will go up in value can buy an option to buy that currency and earn big money if they turn out to be right. When the Swiss franc rises, anyone holding a Swiss franc call—which gives them the right to buy the Swiss franc for less—will profit.

Likewise, if a currency goes down against the dollar, an option to sell that currency—a put option—would become more valuable. A Texas computer manufacturer anticipating big sales in Switzerland, for example, could buy a Swiss franc put option to "lock in" the U.S. dollar value of the sale. This "hedge" would insure against any unanticipated losses if the value of the Swiss franc were to drop before the computers are sold in Geneva and Zurich.

Exporters and anyone who trades in the world economy, in fact, often need to know in advance what their bottom line will be, in their own currency. Therefore, most companies, even small ones, use currency options to prevent earnings from being affected by unanticipated currency fluctuations. With global trade now contributing substantially to many companies' profits, the use of currency options allows for trade to grow, unencumbered by the use of many different currencies used around the world.

47. WHAT IS A HEDGE FUND?

HEDGE FUNDS GET their name from the practice of "hedging": using securities or investment strategies to ensure that one investment's gain counteracts another investment's loss.

Modern hedge funds, however, have evolved from conservative portfolios of investments to highly speculative, highly volatile global funds.

Most hedge funds make a profit by borrowing enormous amounts of money to pay for speculative investments—usually in parts of the world economy that banks and other traditional investors shy away from. Hedge funds have become so big that the U.S. Federal Reserve has had to step in, on occasion, to bail them out.

In the late 1990s, for example, the collapse of Long-Term Capital Management's hedge fund threatened to upset the global financial system when it was discovered that several banks and securities houses had loaned the hedge fund enormous amounts of money—and probably weren't going to get their money back. Some hedge funds, however, have had spectacular success investing in such areas as Russian currency markets, oil prices, or yield differentials between different kinds of U.S. Treasury bonds.

Hedge funds can earn billions, or lose billions, overnight—often through the use of computer models that oversee a complex web of interrelated investments. By borrowing large amounts of money, hedge funds can invest in a wide variety of bonds, commodities, currencies, and stocks around the world—always attempting to "beat the market." When speculators are all moving in one direction, often a hedge fund will step in to exploit discrepancies in the markets and take "bets" on a different direction for the markets.

48. WHAT IS HOT MONEY?

IT HAS BEEN said that a butterfly flapping its wings over Tokyo could cause a rainstorm over New York's Central Park several days later. Events in the world economy are also interconnected, except that the markets in the Far East do not have to wait several days before reacting to changes in New York or London.

In the new global economy, events occur almost simultaneously. If the NASDAQ loses ten percent of its value in New York, high-tech markets around the world plunge immediately. And when a developing country, such as Ecuador or Malaysia, defaults on its international loans, investors from around the world may pull billions of dollars out of other, relatively healthy economies without batting an eyelash.

Hot money, also called "smart money," refers to the trillions of dollars that are invested on a short-term basis in markets around the world. When markets change, this money can come flowing into and out of an economy at a moment's notice. All it takes is an electronic transfer order to send billions of dollars flowing from one part of the globe to another. Hot money managers are usually the first to react to any news in the global economy.

Political changes, such as an assassination or a surprising election result, and economic changes, such as a plan to seize foreign assets or a new interest-rate policy, can cause currency or stock markets around the world to decline—or rise—precipitously.

Although hot money is usually managed by big banks or investment houses, it actually represents the savings and investments of individual investors. Hot money ranges from a New York–based fund investing in Indonesia to a New Delhi corporation buying Eurobonds in London. With the World Wide Web and international news services bringing information onto bank trading floors and into living rooms from Johannesburg to Jamaica, investors are immediately aware of any change that may affect their life's savings. For example the California Public Employees Retirement Fund, one of the world's largest single investors, has billions of dollars to invest in the world's markets at any given time. Its decision to move in or out of a particular market affects markets abroad as well as the financial well-being of retirees at home.

Like the butterfly flapping its wings over Tokyo, even small investment decisions can affect the global marketplace. When an investor in California decides to sell shares in a fund that invests in Latin America, that decision sets in motion a chain of events that can be felt even in a small village in Chile. By giving the order to redeem $100,000 of an emerging-market equity fund, for example, the investor and others making the same decision force the fund manager to sell some of the shares in order to pay off the departing clients. These shares might be for a small mining company in the south of Chile, and when the "sell" order comes into the Santiago stock exchange, it has an effect on the stock price. As more investors "get on the bandwagon"— selling off even more of the company's shares—the company may be forced to react, possibly even laying off employees in an effort to become more profitable and regain investors' favor.

At the same time, the money pulled out of Argentina may end up—within minutes—invested in a Dutch dot-com startup, or a Chinese telephone company, or U.S. Treasuries. With a few simple transactions, banks and securities traders can easily move hundreds of billions of dollars per day from one part of the world to another.

The total amount of hot money moving into and out of economies around the world can dwarf the total economy of most countries in the world. For comparison's sake, the value of all the world's gold mined since King Solomon's day is estimated to be only a small fraction of the value of investments in the world's derivatives markets on any given day.

Like all financial investors, the owners of this speculative flood of money are simply looking for a favorable return on their investment. Essentially, they are looking for countries that have sound financial policies, reasonable prospects for growth, and, in the end, profit.

Some world leaders have called for the imposition of laws to stop these speculative flows of hot money, arguing that they are responsible for political and social upheaval. Some have even called for the imposition of special taxes on hot money flows. One example is the so-called "Tobin Tax," named after the Nobel Prize–winning economist who proposed it, James Tobin. This special tax would be applied to global flows and provide money for "social" investment in the Third World. Access to global capital, however, can often do more good for the developing world than handouts from rich countries or banks (see *What Is the Third World?*).

49. WHAT IS THE NEW ECONOMY?

JUST AS THE invention of trains allowed the world economy to increase its output significantly at the end of the nineteenth century, the "digital revolution" of computers and Web-based business has completely transformed today's global economy.

This paradigm shift, or change in the rules of the game, is based on new ways of producing and trading goods and services. While the invention of the train affected only how fast goods and people could be moved from one place to another, the Internet has transformed the way goods and services are produced, in addition to the way they are delivered.

The New Economy is, above all, based on rapid gains in *productivity.* For every hour that an employee works, the output of goods and services has increased enormously, mainly because of technological advances and more efficient ways of doing business. New means of communication, new means of distribution, and new competition from other parts of the world have all contributed to this rise in productivity. In the United States, productivity grew almost three percent per year between the years 1995 and 2000. This was more than double the average growth in productivity over the previous twenty-five years.

These gains were, in part, helped by the end of the Cold War and lower oil costs, but it is hard to deny that a true revolution has occurred. The productivity gains from information technology and the Internet may be more far-reaching than the invention of electric power, the telephone, or the internal combustion engine.

The New Economy tends to be *disinflationary* in the sense that technological advances have made increased growth possible without rising prices. This is referred to by economists as "a shift of the supply curve to the right," which simply means that producers can produce more—and consumers can buy more—without pushing prices higher. Large increases in productivity also mean larger company profit margins and increasing tax revenues, which have led to higher government surpluses worldwide.

The Internet has also made it possible for small businesses to become more efficient. Farmers, for example, who used to rely on the newspaper for weather information, can now use the Web to get up-to-the-minute information on the latest weather forecasts. They can also use the Web to get agronomic advice and risk-management tools that were previously reserved for the elite. They can also access markets on the Web, using Web-based exchanges to buy pesticides and fertilizers at lower prices, or even find new buyers for their crops. This all translates into increased production and lower prices for the end user, the consumer.

The Internet also provides a needed boost to the emerging economies of the world. Small businesses in the Third World that used to sell their goods through big multinational trading groups can now access the world market directly. An automobile parts firm in South Korea can now sell directly to a factory in Detroit, or a dressmaker in India or Guatemala can sell to a dress shop in Chicago—or directly to consumers who have provided a body scan over the Web. Instead of waiting years or decades for new ideas to filter down to them, businesses and consumers in developing countries can now have instant access to new technologies and markets, making them more efficient and more profitable.

This brings us to the downside of the New Economy: economic growth in other parts of the world often means competition for businesses at home. Even though economic growth means a higher standard of living for most members of the world economy, some people do lose jobs, especially those who lack the training to take part in the high-tech revolution. In Silicon Valley, for example, the lowest paid employees—including secretaries—saw real income fall by almost ten percent between 1990 and 2000, while dot-com billionaires saw their net worth soar.

One of the goals of the European Union in calling for a

high-tech revolution of its own was to ensure that it is based more on "fairness," providing more access to jobs for all, not just the technological elite. Whether this is compatible with the New Economy "miracle" remains to be seen. Certainly one essential step to more equality in the New Economy is to increase training in schools and retraining for adults who have lost their jobs. Widespread digital literacy will be a *sine qua non* for any country trying to make its way in the New Economy.

Another concern is that New Economy companies will use their technological advantage to secure a monopoly on a particular industry. This was the thinking behind the U.S. government's anti-trust suit against Microsoft. In truth, the Internet generally tends to reduce barriers to entry. In most businesses, the Internet has made it easier for companies to move into a market and set up shop, providing ready competition to any firm trying to corner the market.

50. HOW CAN NEW ECONOMY COMPANIES BE COMPARED TO TRADITIONAL COMPANIES?

LIKE A YOUNG fruit tree with many years of harvest to come, a company's shares are evaluated by estimating the company's profits over the years to come. The problem in judging New Economy stocks is that many companies resemble saplings, in that they have no earnings.

How do you judge a company that has no profits in sight? Traditionally, a company's share price is related to its past earnings, or profit. A company's *price/earnings ratio* (p/e) is obtained by dividing current price by current earnings. When a company's earnings increase, its share price often rises in tandem, keeping its p/e ratio in line with other companies within its industry. By buying a stock with a p/e ratio of 10, an investor of a traditional company makes a thumbnail assessment that the company's earnings will pay for the share's price in ten years' time.

When a company has no earnings at all, however, it is necessary to look at other factors. At the beginning of the high-tech stock boom during the 1990s, many investors decided to throw reason to the wind and invest in whichever stock looked as though it would be the market leader. The rationale behind this "first mover" analysis was that the New Economy would provide a totally new environment—a new paradigm where the traditional rules no longer applied. The subsequent crash of many of the dot-com stocks brought investors back to more traditional methods of valuing stocks, placing a premium on the ones that would show some profit, at least in the near future.

A valuable tool for judging a New Economy company without profits is to look at its revenue flow. A company's *price/revenue ratio* (p/r) is based on the concept that a company's price should have some relation to the amount of sales that a company is generating. A p/r ratio, as the name implies, is obtained by dividing current price by current revenue. A more finely tuned method of judging a company's value is to look at its cash flow. The price to cash flow ratio shows investors the relationship between a stock price and the company's "real" income.

It is also important to look at how New Economy companies are funded. Since many Internet companies have never shown a profit, they often prefer to get money by issuing new shares—usually through an Initial Public Offering (see *What Is an IPO?*). Some high-tech startups, such as Amazon.com, have also issued bonds that are convertible into stocks at a fixed price. These *convertible bonds* provide investors with a constant cash flow from the bond's interest payments and, in addition, allow them to take advantage of a future rise in the company's share price. Most convertible bonds are essentially equity investments.

In a global context, comparing New and Old Economy companies is made even more difficult by the use of different currencies and different methods of evaluating earnings. Many countries, for example, have radically different accounting rules that come up with substantially different earnings statements. In a country where depreciation is more easily allowed—in Japan, for example—companies will show lower earnings than in countries where they are required to state the full value of their income.

What makes New Economy stocks especially difficult to evaluate is the fact that they are part of a totally new line of business. In a more mature business sector, it is easier to tell which companies are going to succeed. In the Internet world, where many companies are truly "startups," it is often still too early to tell.

Another way of judging New Economy stocks is to try to anticipate what the economic environment will be like in the years to come. Some economists point out that the companies that make the biggest profits are those that are able to take advantage of economic scarcities. During the early stages of modern economic growth, for example, there was a scarcity of power and a lot of land, such as in the American West. In that economic environment, the steamship and railroad companies prospered. During the twentieth century, when land was becoming scarcer, the oil and real estate companies profited enormously. At the dawn of the twenty-first century, the major scarcity appears to be time. Those companies that allow businesses and consumers to reduce the amount of time spent—for everything from online shopping to sending large quantities of digital information halfway around the world—may be in the best position to profit from the new economic environment.

Other economists point out that there is no real difference between New Economy and Old Economy companies, that many e-commerce businesses earn their money the "old-fashioned" way, by charging a fee for customers to use proprietary technology. E-bay, for example, has set up a computer-guided auction system that basically works on its own: the customers do all the buying and selling, and E-bay just collects a fee. In this way, an Internet technology company is similar to a traditional telephone company that has built the infrastructure and simply charges its customers a fee to use it.

Other Internet companies get their revenues from ads, not from the core business. In this way, they can be compared to a magazine or a TV broadcaster that uses content to attract customers, earning money from commercials.

Some "e-tailers," such as Amazon.com, sell over the Internet but still have to build a bricks-and-mortar infrastructure to stock merchandise, package it, and then ship it to customers around the world. How different are they from Sears or Wal-Mart, which also sell goods over the Web?

Basically, the New Economy is blurring boundaries between different types of companies. Traditional manufacturers and e-tailers are both doing business on each other's turf. Consumers are using the Web to buy automobiles directly from the factory, while traditional retailers, such as Barnes & Noble, have set up Web sites of their own to compete directly with the online upstarts.

51. WHAT IS E-COMMERCE?

THE INTERNET PROVIDES for the world's first "friction-free" marketplace in the sense that business and consumers from around the world can use it for transactions without the overhead and inefficiencies of traditional bricks-and-mortar offices. Bank transfers, for example, cost the bank more than a dollar if done by a teller, about 25 cents if done by a cash machine, and less than a cent if done over the Internet.

By the end of the twentieth century, business transacted on the Internet, usually referred to as *e-commerce,* was growing at over a hundred percent a year. With Internet access provided by everything from cell phones to steering wheels, consumers and business finally had complete access to the global marketplace. When the U.S. government—and other governments around the world—allowed contracts signed on the Internet to have the same legal status as a contract signed on paper, any kind of transaction became possible. Virtually every form of business can now be conducted on the Web: from issuing insurance policies to buying a house to watching a pay-for-view pornographic movie.

Most e-commerce takes place between businesses. This "B2B" marketplace initially was made up of companies setting up online exchanges to buy materials and other products from each other. These *eHubs* or *eMarketplaces* provide a wider range of trading partners, leading to lower prices and increased productivity for the businesses that use them. The major U.S. carmakers, for example, have joined forces to create a B2B site that would allow them to buy billions of dollars of parts and other products from thousands of suppliers scattered across the globe. This quickly led to lower costs, and not just because it was easier to find cheaper suppliers. B2B exchanges generally allow better control over supply and inventory, so companies can save on inventory overhead and administration costs.

The cost savings from B2B commerce were immediately felt throughout the world economy. The rules of the game had changed: companies could produce more and more without having to raise prices. By going online, even small companies found they could buy supplies and "indirect inputs" such as electricity or telephone services at a lower cost by pooling their purchases with other buyers in the same industry.

Business to consumer e-commerce (B2C) started even before B2B e-commerce, when online retailers, such as Amazon.com or Schwab.com, created billion-dollar industries by providing consumers with products and services that were cheaper and easier to get on the Web. The Internet also allowed sellers to offer tailor-made products. Consumers could use the Web to order a watch, for example, that exactly fit their specifications—from size to color to the kind of numbers on the dial. Henry Ford once said customers could buy his Model-T in "any color you want, as long as it's black." Now, Ford gives customers online a complete view of every car regional dealers have in stock, including information on what car models are on order and which cars are being built.

This openness and transparency of the Web have also helped the developing countries in their efforts to overcome the hurdles of inadequate infrastructure, such as poor communications and storage facilities. Doing business online allows companies in Third World countries to compete on a global scale, and having business dealings online, in full view of everyone, can also help reduce corruption around the world.

Most of the world's e-commerce markets have yet to be

tapped. Only 2 percent of China's population had a computer in the year 2000, for example, compared to more than 50 percent in the United States. And of those who had computers in China, only 20 percent had access to the Internet. As soon as the billions of people in the developing countries of the world are brought online, the e-commerce revolution will really begin.

52. WHAT IS THE EUROPEAN UNION?

UNITING A CONTINENT with more than forty countries and almost as many languages, currencies, cultures, and political systems is not an easy task. Apart from brief periods of pan-European military rule—such as during the Roman or the Napoleonic empires—Europe has been divided by political and ethnic barriers that defied countless attempts at unification. England, for example, has often preferred to maintain closer relations with its former colonies around the world than with its European neighbors. Other countries, such as Norway and Switzerland, have sought to preserve their independence at all costs.

In the last years of the twentieth century, however, the continent of Europe has been completely transformed. The fall of the Soviet Bloc, which had divided the continent for almost a half a century, provided an opportunity for Europe to unite in a way that it had never imagined before.

The quest for European economic unity has involved three distinct groups of countries: the members of the European Union (EU); the Western European countries that opted not to

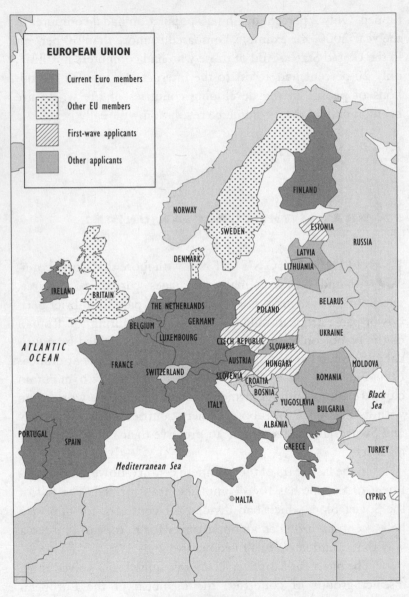

EUROPE

join the EU; and the formerly communist countries in Central and Eastern Europe. Uniting these nations would produce the most powerful economic bloc in the world. With a population of more than 700 million people and a total economic output exceeding that of China, Japan, or the United States, an integrated Europe truly would become an economic superpower.

The European Union had its beginnings in 1957 when six countries—Belgium, France, the Netherlands, Italy, Luxembourg, and West Germany—signed the Treaty of Rome to form the European Coal and Steel Community, later called the European Economic Community (EEC), or simply, the "Common Market." As the trade group grew during the 1970s and 1980s to include Britain, Ireland, Denmark, Greece, Spain, and Portugal, the original treaties were expanded to cover a wide range of political, agricultural, industrial, and monetary agreements, including the Common Agricultural Policy (CAP) that guaranteed large subsidies to European farmers.

In the mid-1990s, after the addition of three new members—Austria, Finland, and Sweden—the name was changed to "European Union"; the common market had finally become a true economic and political union. The decision to remove all barriers to people, goods, and money was formalized in the Dutch town of Maastricht, which came to symbolize the drive for a unified Europe. After Maastricht citizens of Portugal were allowed to live and work anywhere from London to Amsterdam to Athens; goods could flow from Sweden to Italy without any extra formalities; and money could be transferred from Madrid to Frankfurt without restrictions.

By the end of the 1990s, the European Union had become the world's most successful free-trade "megazone" (see *What Are Free-Trade Megazones?*). Citizens in some EU countries, called the "Schengen Zone" after another Dutch town where the treaty was signed, agreed to remove borders completely, removing the requirement for a passport check as people passed from one country to another.

The introduction of the euro in 1999 meant true barrier-free trade among the eleven EU countries that decided to adopt the common currency. The only euro-holdouts were Denmark, Sweden, and the UK (see *What Is the Euro?*). The Treaty of Nice, signed in December 2000, also removed the requirement for unanimity in much of the EU–decision-making, allowing for the enlargement of the EU to include up to thirteen new members from Central and Eastern Europe.

It was decided to allow the healthiest economies in first. The first wave of new members would include Poland, Hungary, and the Czech Republic. These three countries had already become part of NATO (the North Atlantic Treaty Organization) in 1999. The other "fast track" entrants were Cyprus, Estonia, and Slovenia. The six new members in the second wave of applicants were: Latvia, Malta, Slovakia, Lithuania, Bulgaria, and Romania. Turkey was initially not invited to become a full member, but was told to prepare for eventual inclusion into the European "club" by making its laws and labor standards conform to those used throughout the European Union.

The only Western European EU-holdouts—Switzerland, Iceland, and Norway—decided to take a "wait and see" policy, choosing to take advantage of access to the EU market through bi-lateral trade agreements without entering the union officially. These relatively wealthy nations had also ensured barrier-free trade among themselves through the European Free Trade Association (EFTA).

53. HOW ARE COMMUNIST COUNTRIES TRANSFORMED BY CAPITALISM?

SOME COMMUNIST COUNTRIES have prospered enormously in their "capitalist" ventures. During the last decades of the twentieth century, for example, the People's Republic of China made one of the fastest climbs out of poverty achieved by any nation in history. After disbanding agricultural communes and sending the people to work in low-wage factories, Communist China was able to build one of the biggest economies in the world. The major question facing the world's communist countries remains: how long can a thriving free-market economy exist under a totalitarian form of government?

The communist system was based on an economic and social theory, developed by Karl Marx in the nineteenth century, that called for a takeover of the state by the workers. This "dictatorship of the proletariat" would, Marx thought, pave the way to true socialism where the pain and inequities of capitalism would be replaced by communism—an economic system where life would be organized on the principle: "from each according to his abilities, to each according to his needs." Instead of letting the markets make the major economic decisions, a communist economy puts decision-making in the hands of the government, in the hopes of creating a more egalitarian "communal" society.

Although communist central planning brought about rapid economic growth in some countries, such as the Soviet Union in the 1920s and 1930s, it has most often resulted in inefficiency and economic stagnation. In Eastern Europe, for example, the communist countries of the Soviet bloc saw their modest growth outstripped by the dazzling wealth and power of their neighbors to the West.

The fall of the Soviet Union in the early 1990s allowed the other communist countries to re-evaluate the benefits of communism. Most countries in Central and Eastern Europe opted to abandon Marxist philosophy and moved quickly toward Western market economies (see *How Is the Former Soviet Bloc Being Integrated into the World Economy?*). By the year 2000, only four major communist countries were left: Vietnam, Cuba, North Korea, and China.

Vietnam decided to attempt to create a new form of communism—one with distinctly capitalist aspects. Under a perestroika-like economic re-awakening, called *doi moi* in Vietnamese, the communist government invited foreign firms to open new factories throughout the country, in hopes of providing employment for more than one million new young people entering the work force each year. The first stock exchange was opened in 2000, albeit with only two stocks trading. Saigon, still officially called Ho Chi Minh City, gradually became a thriving capitalist city with private ownership of everything from apartments to motorbikes.

Cuba, faced with a trade embargo imposed unilaterally by the United States, turned to Latin America and Europe for trade and investment. Unfortunately, its economy was in ruins. Tourism slowly began to grow, however, and soon foreigners from Canada, Europe, and Latin America were filling the newly built resort hotels. Despite a desire to show its independence from its powerful neighbor to the north, Cuba adopted a parallel "U.S. dollar" economy where those with access to foreigners and their dollars were allowed to eat in special "dollar" restaurants and shop in "dollar" stores. The poor underclass, with the almost worthless *pesos normales,* were kept out. Paradoxically, this division of economic classes was precisely what communism was supposed to abolish.

At the dawn of the new millennium, North Korea faced economic collapse and widespread famine. The semi-feudal Stalinist economy had forced the government to become a global beggar: the only thing keeping the country alive was relief food from China, South Korea, and several wealthy Western countries, including the United States and Canada. Desperately in need of money to revive its antiquated farms, factories, and power grid, North Korea turned to its brother-republic to the South, proposing talks aimed at eventual reunification. In an effort to begin rebuilding the north, executives from South Korea's largest industrial conglomerates, or *chaebols,* moved to set up industrial zones within the communist north, bringing in hundreds of new manufacturing plants to provide work for North Korea's relatively low-paid workers.

China had already set the pattern for planting capitalist seeds within a communist economy. By the end of the twentieth century, the People's Republic of China had become one of the biggest capitalist economies of the world. Across the country, factories, farms, and homes had returned to private hands. The economy was growing at double-digit rates, lifting more than 200 million people—equivalent to the entire population of the United States—out of poverty over the course of two decades. The sharp fall in the Chinese birth rate, to about 1.3 percent per year, also helped enormously.

China's communist leaders said they hoped for a return to *fuqiang*—a Mandarin word meaning "rightful prosperity and power." In many ways, they succeeded: Hong Kong and Macau were absorbed into the country as "special economic zones," with their own local governments and economic systems. In other economic growth zones, especially in the south, prosperity was easy to see—privately owned houses and factories were appearing everywhere. Rapid economic growth brought China's economy to such a level of prosperity that it was invited to join the World Trade Organization. In the year 2000, it was granted Permanent Normal Trade Relations (PNTR) status with the United States. China's aging communist leaders, however, faced a dilemma. How could they continue providing the economic freedom that would allow the country to grow even further while retaining central political and economic control?

The debate in China, as in the other Communist countries trying to integrate themselves into the capitalist economic system, centers on how much the people can be allowed to do economically, without opening the doors to political freedom. Democracy, one of the main demands of the students killed by government troops in Tiananmen Square in 1989, is often one of the first requests from citizens who have been given a taste of economic freedom.

54. HOW IS THE FORMER SOVIET BLOC BEING INTEGRATED INTO THE WORLD ECONOMY?

WHEN THE COMMUNIST countries of the Soviet bloc decided to abandon more than fifty years of socialism and join the capitalist West, their worst-case scenario began with economics, not politics. One of their worst fears was that painful economic restructuring would lead to social unrest.

This fear was quickly reinforced by a failed old-guard

coup in Russia, followed by revolts in several former Soviet republics. Even in relatively wealthy East Germany, and despite all the billions of marks of aid from the West, many people yearned for a return to the "good old days" of communism when jobs were secure and social services were all paid for by the state.

As the countries of Central and Eastern Europe were transforming their economies during the 1990s, they had one thing in mind: joining the European Union. Central planning quickly gave way to "transition economics" in most Eastern European countries. From Poland to Slovenia the old Iron Curtain lifted to reveal more than a dozen countries eager to join their free-market neighbors to the west. However, the transition was often hindered by crumbling infrastructure and extremely high unemployment resulting from the closing of inefficient state-owned industries.

Instead of moving immediately to completely free-market economies, some countries chose a middle road, where governments would still provide a vast economic safety net. This hybrid system was inspired, in part, by the "Third Way" economic policies of Britain and Sweden, which had been relatively successful in combining the advantages of socialism with the dynamism of the free market.

Other countries opted to move quickly and made an immediate transition to capitalism. The Federal Republic of Germany's decision to transform East Germany into a fully functioning capitalist economy was a prime example. Huge investments in infrastructure, such as highways and telephone systems, as well as the complete restructuring of inefficient industries put enormous drain on the resources of one of the world's richest countries.

Even with all the resources of the Federal Republic at its

disposal, it took many years for East Germany to even begin to resemble the successful capitalist economies of the EU. Imagine, then, the difficulties faced by the other Central European economies as they began their long journey to adapt European Union norms and business methods in every sector of the economy.

Despite their efforts, the rich countries already inside the EU hesitated to admit the newcomers too quickly. Some countries, such as Poland, Hungary, and the Czech Republic, had to initially settle for NATO membership, which succeeded in providing a certain level of security for foreign investors.

Further to the east, Russia made it clear it had no intention of joining either NATO or the European Union. The European Union was, in a way, relieved. With eighty-nine component provinces and regions stretching from the Baltic to the Pacific, Russia was considered by many Europeans to be a continent in itself.

When Vladimir Putin took power at the beginning of the twenty-first century, one of his first steps was to begin fighting the violence, autocracy, and corruption that had taken over the Russian economy. He faced the painful decision of allowing Russia to become a true free-market economy, with currency convertibility and an end to price controls, or remain a semi-privatized economy. Most of the other former members of the Soviet Bloc had already decided that the only way to overcome the decades of economic mismanagement was a complete transition to free-market economies—despite the difficult period of economic austerity this path would require.

55. WHAT ARE THE TIGER ECONOMIES OF SOUTHEAST ASIA?

TAKING THEIR CUE from Japan, the economies of South Korea, Singapore, Taiwan, and Hong Kong—followed closely by Indonesia, Malaysia, and Thailand—chose to base their growth on exports. By the mid-1990s, these "Tiger economies" had made such rapid economic growth that they had all been included in the select group of advanced developing economies referred to as "Newly Industrialized Countries" (NICs).

The Asia Crisis in 1997, however, brought several Southeast Asian countries to the brink of economic collapse. Currencies tumbled, foreign investors bailed out, and banks began to fail as companies everywhere were going bankrupt. Even though the region's self-confidence was shaken—some say *because* it was shaken—the countries of Southeast Asia looked for new ways of doing things. Instead of hoping for another "Asian Miracle," most Southeast Asian leaders began the painful work of economic and political transformation—even, in some cases, removing longtime dictators.

The new governments worked to quickly put an end to the corrupt business practices of the past. In Indonesia, for example, the acronym KKN, standing for *korupse, kolusi, nepotisme* in Bahasa, had been used to refer to the corruption, collusion, and nepotism that had long been accepted as part of any budding Asian economy. The new government promised that things would now be done differently.

Many Southeast Asian economies were also helped by the

fact that their newly devalued currencies made exports much less expensive on the world markets. Shipments of toys, clothes, and machinery surged as economies from Hong Kong to Thailand got back to work. Despite the critics' charge that the U.S. Treasury and the IMF (International Monetary Fund) had overemphasized economic restructuring and fiscal austerity in their $100 billion bailout, the proof that their "tough love" had worked was easily seen in the booming export growth in many of the resurgent Tiger economies.

Another grouping of the Southeast Asian economies is ASEAN: the Association of Southeast Asian Nations. ASEAN members include Indonesia, the world's largest Muslim country, with more than 200 million inhabitants; the oil-rich Sultanate of Brunei; not-so-communist Vietnam; the rapidly growing economies of Thailand, Singapore, and the Philippines; and the relatively poor countries of Cambodia, Laos, and Myanmar, commonly referred to as Burma.

56. WHAT IS JAPAN INC.?

AT THE END of the twentieth century, Japan found itself contemplating the prospect of a wide range of social and economic reforms. Despite a huge current account surplus, the country was going through one of the longest recessions in its history. Several consecutive quarters of negative growth—almost unheard of in modern industrial economies—had burdened banks with trillions of yen in bad debts as companies and individuals went bankrupt at unprecedented rates. Even golf

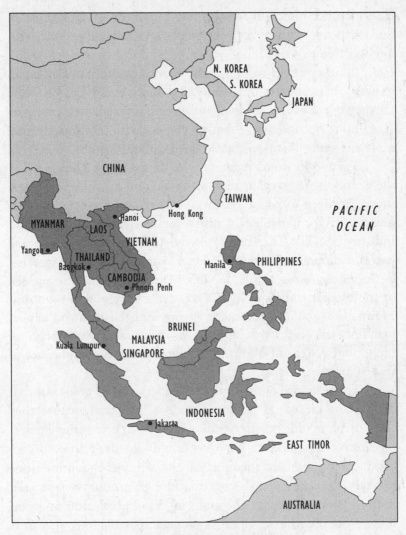

SOUTHEAST ASIA

club memberships, which had cost hundreds of thousands of dollars to acquire during the booming 1980s, had become virtually worthless.

In an effort to stimulate the economy, the Bank of Japan reduced interest rates drastically. But there was a limit to how far they could go. When they got to an unprecedented zero percent and the economy still hadn't responded, there was nothing more the central bank could do but wait and watch.

The world wondered what had happened to "Japan Inc.," the economic juggernaut that was based on a "common enterprise" between Japanese business leaders and politicians, coordinated by the Japanese Ministry for International Trade and Industry (MITI). The success of the Japanese export machine had not diminished, however. Even with the economy in crisis during most of the 1990s, Japan still succeeded in creating one of the biggest trade surpluses ever seen in the global economy. Many global competitors were saying that the Japanese export machine had been working a bit *too* well, taking advantage of the global system of free trade while keeping a complex set of trade barriers at home.

The response of the Japanese leaders was to point out that the rest of the world bought Japanese products because they were better made and, above all, were sold at competitive prices on the world markets. But they could not deny that foreign products in Japan did encounter a vast series of Byzantine trade barriers. Finding a distributor for a foreign product is especially hard in Japan because of the many layers of protectionism stemming from the practice of cross-ownership, called *keiretsu*. It is common, for example, for many Japanese stores to only sell the products from within the store's group. Loyalty to one's *keiretsu* often overshadows any desire to buy cheaper products from outside.

The Internet began putting this practice to the test, however. By increasing price transparency, the Internet gave power to consumers to make their own decisions about which products to buy. It was no longer necessary to go through the inefficient system of distributors that dominate the Japanese economy.

In the same way that the Japanese economy was forced to open up to foreign trade when Commander Perry sailed into Tokyo Bay in the nineteenth century, today's leaders have been forced to change the old way of doing things. After deregulating the economy and reforming the financial system, banks, and businesses, Japan has suddenly found itself even more competitive than under the paternalist system known as Japan Inc.

57. WHAT IS THE THIRD WORLD?

THE TERM THIRD World was originally devised to describe the poor, or "developing," countries of the world. It was based on the idea that the "first" and "second" worlds consisted of the free-market economies and the centrally planned "socialist" economies in Europe, North America, and Asia. In recent years, the Third World economies have also come to be referred to as "emerging markets" or "developing economies." Essentially, the countries of the Third World can be divided into three groups: those developing rapidly, those developing moderately, and the poorest few, whose economies are not developing at all.

At the top of the list are the rapidly developing countries called *Newly Industrialized Countries* (NICs). Most lists of the

Newly Industrialized Countries include Argentina, Brazil, Chile, Mexico, Singapore, South Africa, South Korea, Taiwan, Thailand, and several countries in Central Europe.

The bulk of the Third World consists of the moderately developing economies, which include most of the countries in Asia and Latin America and some of the African countries. The most populous countries in this group are: China, India, Indonesia, and Malaysia (see *How Are Communist Countries Transformed by Capitalism?* and *What Are the Tiger Economies of Southeast Asia?*).

At the bottom of the list are the world's poorest countries, or Less Developed Countries (LDCs), that have so few resources and so little money that it is virtually impossible for them to develop their economies at all. Most of the countries in this list are found in sub-Saharan Africa. In Somalia and Niger, for example, there are virtually no resources on which to base economic growth. Other countries in this group are prevented from joining the rest of the "developed" world by a variety of factors such as chronic warfare, corrupt governments, and health crises such as AIDS (see *What Is the Effect of the AIDS Epidemic on the World Economy?*). This group of stagnating countries is also sometimes referred to as the "Fourth World," or "Highly Indebted Poor Countries" (HIDCs).

Although the Third World comprises three quarters of the world's population and is responsible for almost all of the world's population growth, it is still only able to produce less than 25 percent of the world's total economic output. (See *What Causes the Income Gap Between Rich and Poor Countries?* and *What Are Economic Austerity Plans?*) Even though the countries of the Third World hold much of the world's natural resources, including vast petroleum and mineral reserves, most of these resources are simply shipped abroad for consumption and use by the world's wealthier and more developed economies.

58. WHAT IS HYPERINFLATION?

DURING A HYPERINFLATIONARY period in Argentina, when the currency was losing its value at an alarming rate, a popular joke was that it was cheaper to take a taxi than a bus because the bus ride was paid for at the beginning, when the currency was still worth something, while the taxi ride was paid for at the end—after the currency had already lost its value.

Hyperinflation, an explosion in the prices of goods and services at rates exceeding 100 percent per year, is a symptom of an economy out of control. Hyperinflation has occurred, at various times, all over the world: in Germany between the two world wars, in Israel, and in various parts of Eastern Europe—especially in the war-torn countries of the Balkans. But hyperinflation has been most widespread in the debtor countries of Latin America, where it resulted primarily from government policies that attempted to satisfy political demands without looking at the economic consequences.

When a profligate government finances spending by increased borrowing abroad or by printing new currency, prices increase as the new funds enter the economy. The result is a vicious circle: the *expectation* of runaway inflation fuels the fires of inflation and the wage/price spiral takes on a life of its own. Prices rise quickly, leading to a demand for increased wages to pay for the increased prices, which leads to even higher prices.

Imagine buying goods for a home or a factory—or playing *The Price is Right*—when prices are increasing at the rate of 30 percent a month. Even winning the lottery may not help when a million—or a billion—pesos doesn't even pay for next month's rent. There were cases in hyperinflationary Germany after

World War I when people had to use a wheelbarrow to bring enough money to buy a day's supply of food.

Hyperinflation's radically rising prices often end up hurting poor people the most, because their day-to-day expenses consume a significantly higher percentage of their total income. Also, rich people have access to bank accounts that pay high rates of interest during times of hyperinflation while poor people rely on cash, which pays no interest, for their daily transactions. Some countries with high inflation therefore try to index all salaries and social service payments to the inflation rate. But this rarely keeps pace with the real increase in prices, and purchasing power declines.

Hyperinflation also hurts those on fixed incomes such as old-age pensions. During inflationary times, a nest egg—if not invested in something that tracks the rising cost of living—is soon worthless (see *What Is Dollarization?*). Many people have seen their savings decimated by hyperinflation.

Governments often refuse to take tough action against hyperinflation because they fear the political consequences of austerity plans or increased taxes. May overburdened governments simply borrow—or print—more money to keep from closing inefficient state industries or reducing bloated bureaucracies. These financial tricks will only work for a while, however, as the self-perpetuating spiral of wage and price increases spins out of control.

Just as a dying patient sometimes needs electroshock therapy to return to the land of the living, a hyperinflationary economy sometimes needs an economic shock to bring it back to health. This shock can take many forms: some are political, some economic. In mid-1990s Brazil, for example, a new government took over during a particularly difficult period of hyperinflation. One of the first things the new president did was appoint a team of economists to come up with a plan to end the economic chaos ravaging the country. Their *plano real* called for a radical departure from the previous way of doing things, including, among other measures, opening up the country to imports and locking the currency into a quasi-fixed rate against the dollar. Consumers were shocked to suddenly find cheaper alternatives to expensive local goods.

Expectations of rising prices fuels hyperinflation as much as rising prices themselves. Increased demand for wage increases puts pressure on companies to raise their prices. By coming up with an economic plan that convinces people that the storm is over, a government has already won half the battle in the fight against hyperinflation. And by ensuring that prices remain low—by allowing free imports from abroad, for example—the end of hyperinflation is assured.

59. WHAT CAUSES THE INCOME GAP BETWEEN RICH AND POOR COUNTRIES?

AS INCREDIBLE AS it may seem, the net worth of the ten wealthiest people in the world is more than the total yearly earnings of everyone living in the world's developing countries.

The New Economy has generated enormous wealth, especially in the rich industrialized countries. But what effect has this wealth had on the world's poorest countries? By the end of the twentieth century, the income gap between the world's richest and poorest countries was actually growing wider.

While some countries were getting incredibly rich, others were struggling just to keep pace—and some were actually getting poorer. Mozambique, for example, had a per capita income of $1,000 per year in 1950; by the end of the twentieth century it was less than $800. Meanwhile, the per capita income in the United States, Japan, and Switzerland had risen from $12,000 to more than $30,000.

The income gap is more than just differences in salaries; it reflects an immense gap in quality of life between the rich and poor countries. In India, more than a third of all women have never been taught to read. In Mexico's poorer states, one child in five drops out of school before the sixth grade. In Nigeria and Kenya, electricity shortages affect the poor areas on a daily basis, depriving hospitals of power during operations. More than a billion people in the world do not have access to clean water. Three times as many lack proper sanitation in their homes. And more than a hundred million school-age children around the world have never seen the inside of a school.

Is globalization at fault? If all the industry and all the business and all the trade in the world were to stop tomorrow, would the world's poor be better off?

Most developing world leaders see economic growth as the best poverty-reduction tool at their disposal. They point to the fact that more people have been lifted out of poverty in the last fifty years than in the previous five hundred. But several major hurdles still need to be overcome.

The first hurdle is the ongoing population explosion in many Third World countries. In some countries, populations are doubling every twenty years, and in many countries a vicious cycle has developed where extreme poverty has forced people to create large families in hope that the children will work and increase family income. But with no economic opportunities available, many families end up moving to already overcrowded cities in a fruitless search for jobs.

Economic and political mismanagement is also behind much of the poverty in the Third World. The enormous Third World debt burden, for example, was the result of developing governments taking the advice of rich-country banks to make a gamble and borrow "cheap" money—hoping to build the infrastructure and big industries that would produce exports to pay back the loans at a later date. Brazil, for example, had one of the highest growth rates in the world during the 1960s and 1970s, and its economy was producing an ever-increasing surplus of food, clothing, and manufactured goods. It had grown from a poor, underdeveloped nation to become the world's eighth largest economy. Then interest rates skyrocketed and rising oil prices forced the country to borrow heavily to pay for increased fuel imports. Severe economic mismanagement led to gyrating inflation rates and economic stagnation.

One solution is for creditor countries to give developing countries a clean slate—by canceling their debt completely. But that still begs the question: how are the poor countries of the world ever going to be able to work their way out of poverty? (See following section).

60. WHAT CAN BE DONE TO PROMOTE THIRD WORLD DEVELOPMENT?

SOME PEOPLE IN rich countries see economic development in the Third World as a worst-case scenario—more people and businesses consuming more energy, driving more cars, producing more waste. The people in the Third World see it differently: they are already living the worst-case scenario, with overcrowded slums in polluted cities, no access to clean water, no basic services such as health care or police protection, and, above all, no jobs. For most people in the Third World, economic growth is the only hope for a better life.

One of the most effective steps in encouraging economic development is to provide markets for people to sell their goods and services. Even though many people in developing countries work for low salaries by Western standards, a factory job is often an essential first step on their way to economic independence. Rich-country consumers, instead of feeling guilty about buying from abroad, should remind themselves that imports from abroad help create jobs in developing countries. However, consumers still have a responsibility to ensure that what they buy from abroad is not the result of workers who have been abused or exploited.

Exports—of everything from rugs to fruit, from tourism to software—mean money coming in, which allows developing countries to import the goods and services that will fuel their future growth. International trade agreements (see *What Are Free-Trade Megazones?*) help to ensure needed markets for developing countries' goods and services.

In the end, increased trade means more jobs. And a job, even a relatively low-paying one by Western standards, is the best hope for a worker to start building a better life. Instead of a handout, a job is a hand-up—often to a better world. The famous humanitarian Albert Schweitzer once said: "Give a starving man a fish and he will eat for a day; give him a fishing pole and he will hunger no more."

A major factor in promoting Third World development is education. Proper job training is a *sine qua non* for any sort of sustainable development, and without proper training for the children of the developing countries there can be no hope for a more equitable distribution of income. Educating girls, for example, has been shown to be the best development investment a country can make. In some developing countries—as incredible as it may seem—millions of girls are not sent to school at all. But statistics show that girls who have had some schooling— even to primary level—are able to increase family income and are also more likely to have children who survive, who are healthy, and who will be given a proper education when they reach school age.

Another way to help reduce Third World poverty is through *debt reduction*. The amount of money that Africa owed the rest of the world in the year 2000 was more than a third of a trillion dollars—four times its total earnings from exports and almost equal to the total African production of goods and services in any given year. Many governments spend more on interest payments than on health and education combined. *Debt servicing*—principal and interest payments on a country's debt—is often the biggest drain on the resources of a developing country. In the year 2000, for example, the poorest nations of the world were spending up to sixty percent of their budgets to service debt on old loans.

The rationale behind debt reduction is to get more money into developing countries so they can invest for the future. Several international organizations have been set up to provide debt-reduction assistance to developing countries. The Lomé Convention, for example, was set up to channel development aid from the European Union to debtor countries, especially those in Africa. The Paris Club also helps governments of debtor nations by *rescheduling,* or delaying repayment of loans until the economy is in better health.

Foreign direct investment (FDI), foreign investment in a

country's economy, has also grown steadily as the world's rich countries see the vast potential for growth in the Third World. This includes "green-field" investments, such as new factories and power plants, and "paper" investments, such as buying shares of existing companies. In India, for example, foreign investors have contributed to economic growth by investing in infrastructure projects, such as electricity generating plants. This has allowed the Indian economy, already one of the biggest software developers in the world, to set up high-tech plants and call-centers in areas where people previously had no access to high-paying jobs. Many countries like India look to infrastructure projects to allow them to leap over the industrial stage of economic evolution—going directly from poor, rural economies to service economies based on "clean" industries such as technology and media.

The Internet is also providing an important boost to developing economies. Even if local populations don't have widespread access to computers and the World Wide Web, businesses in many developing countries have discovered that having access to consumers and businesses around the world means profit, growth, and jobs. A rug-maker in Nepal, for example, can use the Web to sell to shops and individuals as far away as Sydney or New York City. Software can be developed in India just as easily—and often more cheaply—as in Silicon Valley. Instead of waiting years or decades for new ideas to filter down to them, people in the developing countries will be able to participate on equal footing with other players in the expanding global economy.

Another example of Internet-related help for Third World development is PlaNet Finance, a virtual bank that channels capital into small-scale businesses in the developing world. The online bank doesn't lend money itself, but acts as a clearing house for microfinance institutions, such as the more than seven thousand "poverty banks" that provide small loans to artisans, farmers, and small businesses in developing countries. PlaNet finance has also developed a rating system to allow rich-country banks to determine the credit worthiness of these local lenders— making it easier for global capital to make its way to small businesses in the developing world.

61. WHAT IS THE WORLD BANK?

WHEN PROTESTERS FILLED the covered streets of Washington, D.C., in the year 2000, the institution they were trying to immobilize was none other than the World Bank, officially called the International Bank for Reconstruction and Development.

The World Bank was founded after World War II and was initially used to channel funds from the United States and other donor nations into the reconstruction of postwar Europe. Its first loans were to rebuild wartorn Holland, Denmark, and France. The World Bank now provides almost all of its loans to countries in the Third World and receives funding from many of the now-wealthy nations it was initially set up to assist.

Facing worldwide protests that charge it is merely a tool for monolithic capitalist corporations, the World Bank has gone to great lengths to stress that almost all of the $30 billion it loans out every year goes to community development and poverty reduction programs in the Third World. It also points to its efforts to fight AIDS and provide money to build schools and train teachers in developing countries, going as far as "subsidizing" families so that children can attend school rather than work.

The World Bank, like other development banks (see *What Are Regional Development Banks?*), borrows money on the international markets at highly advantageous rates. This is possible because the World Bank has the implicit backing of rich countries such as Japan and the United States. For example, when the European Union contributes a billion dollars, the World Bank uses this capital to borrow 20 billion dollars by issuing bonds on the world's capital markets. This money can then be lent to projects in the developing world at extremely favorable rates.

In the past, many World Bank loans were criticized for contributing to environmental destruction. Building a dam and a highway system in the Amazon, for example, may have provided economic growth for some, but it ended up opening up vast areas for farming—leading to the destruction of large swaths of virgin rain forest.

The World Bank has gradually moved away from big construction projects and more toward community development. In 1999, it modified lending programs in the Third World, renaming them the "Poverty Reduction and Growth Facility." By providing funds for education projects and small-business loans, the World Bank hoped to do more to alleviate poverty than building dams. The idea was to help developing countries grow incrementally, encouraging small businesses' growth by providing the the infrastructure to allow them to compete with other countries in the world economy.

62. WHAT IS THE IMF?

LIKE A DOCTOR called in at the last minute, the International Monetary Fund (IMF) tries to resuscitate ailing economies, often by prescribing painful financial reform and economic austerity (see *What Are Economic Austerity Plans?*).

The IMF-mandated "structural adjustment" process is often a crucial first step before countries can receive assistance from other sources. When the Asian economies entered an economic free-fall in the late 1990s, the IMF stepped in with an injection of emergency funds and linked further assistance to a rigid program of economic reform.

The IMF, like its sister institution, the World Bank, was founded just after World War II. Both organizations are based in Washington, D.C. Generally, the IMF supervises the world economy and provides last resort funding to economies in need while the World Bank provides funds for economic growth. A related IMF organization, the International Finance Corporation (IFC), also provides low-interest loans to small businesses and other profit-generating companies in the Third World.

Although many people criticize the IMF for prescribing the bitter pill of fiscal austerity when a country is facing economic ruin, the economic shock is often the only thing that revives a moribund economy. The radical restructuring of South Korea's debt-ridden conglomerates, for example, could only occur during a major crisis and only when an external force such as the IMF insisted on it. Most governments are too weak or too linked to local business interest to undertake painful restructuring on their own.

The economic medicine frequently prescribed by the IMF is, in fact, painful. For instance, the IMF often requires debtor governments to reduce subsidies to inefficient state industries and restructure the economy. These measures often provoke unrest, as they often end up raising the cost of previously subsidized services such as bread, milk, and mass transit. During this difficult restructuring process, the IMF often provides temporary "standby" loans to keep the country afloat until more long-term financing can be arranged.

Acceptance of an IMF plan is usually seen as a sign that a nation is prepared to seriously address its economic ills, paving the way for long-term funding from the World Bank and other sources, including individual governments such as the United States or the European Union.

63. WHAT ARE ECONOMIC AUSTERITY PLANS?

WHEN THE U.S. Treasury or the IMF are called upon to help a struggling economy, the first thing they usually insist on is an *economic austerity plan*. These plans usually call for a reduction in government subsidies, which often ends up hurting the poor much more than the rich.

In many struggling debtor countries, the goods and services restricted under economic austerity plans are often those that are most important for a poor person's daily survival. Fuel and foodstuffs are often the first items to have their prices raised in belt-tightening moves. During the Asian Crisis of the late

1990s, for example, several countries were forced to raise interest rates to prop up their ailing currencies—which led to massive economic slowdowns (see *How Are Interest Rates Used to Control Economic Growth?*).

These austerity plans are often criticized for concentrating on paying off creditors first and worrying about the health of people later. In the middle of the Asian Crisis, the IMF actually reversed course—and called for lower interest rates—when it saw the crisis was worsening.

The *structural adjustment plans* that are often prescribed during an economic crisis require the debtor country to reduce domestic consumption of goods, such as shoes or orange juice, in order to send more abroad, thus earning enough foreign currency to pay the outstanding debt.

In addition to reducing government subsidies, many economic austerity plans call for a removal of price controls, allowing the prices for basic foodstuffs, for example, to rise with inflation. At the same time, wages are sometimes frozen, which produces an effective "wage cut." Rising prices mean less purchasing power, especially for the poorest members of society. In addition, if the currency is devalued, it becomes even more expensive to import basic commodities such as flour and fuel.

These steps often lead to civil unrest. During the late 1990s, for example, riots in the poor quarters of Cairo and outright rebellion by peasants in southern Mexico were direct consequences of economic austerity plans.

Many plans imposed by the International Monetary Fund have improved life for people in the developing countries over the long run. But in most debt-ridden economies it is extremely difficult for people to bear the short-term burdens required by austerity plans. Since many of the Third World poor are already living at subsistence levels, a small increase in the cost of essential goods can mean economic disaster. It is not very difficult to go without a new refrigerator—but it is very difficult to go without the food to put in it.

64. WHAT IS DOLLARIZATION?

IF YOU CAN'T beat 'em, join 'em. Faced with the pain of uncontrolled currency fluctuations, some troubled economies have opted to forego a national currency altogether. Panama, for example, has long used the U.S. dollar for all transactions. Faced with economic chaos at the end of the twentieth century, Ecuador and El Salvador also joined the ranks of countries that abandoned their own currencies and moved to a completely dollar-based economy.

Dollarization, replacing the local currency by the dollar, is usually a last resort solution, only put in place when an economy is suffering from extreme inflation (see *What Is Hyperinflation?*) or economic meltdown.

Some countries prefer taking a middle road, using a "currency board" to peg the value of the local currency to a more stable currency such as the euro or the U.S. dollar. In the early 1990s, for example, Argentina established a currency board that issued pesos only when an equal amount of U.S. dollars were put on deposit at the Central Bank. In that way, the Argentine government effectively dollarized the economy, even though the official currency was still the peso.

By eliminating exchange rate fluctuations, currency boards can be an effective defense against foreign speculators. By the year 2000, this system had been put into effect in such disparate countries as Hong Kong, Bulgaria, Estonia, and Lithuania. In Estonia, a currency board was used to link the local currency, the kroon, to the German mark and consequently to the euro. Just as Argentina had chosen the dollar, the Estonians decided that its major trading partners, including Germany, would all be euro-area countries, so every kroon in circulation was backed by a fixed amount of euros. This meant that Estonia had become the first country to be a de facto euro-area member—without even being a member of the European Union.

Other countries have also adopted a de facto currency. In Cuba, for example, by the end of the twentieth century, the dollar had become a second currency. Many "dollar shops" and restaurants were refusing to accept the Cuban peso at all. In Montenegro, the decision to adopt the German mark as the national currency was seen as a sign of economic and political independence from the other parts of Yugoslavia.

Many countries still find it difficult to give up the advantages of having a locally controlled currency. Without the ability to increase the money supply or lower interest rates, there is not much a dollarized country or a country with a currency board can do to stimulate the economy during a difficult economic downturn.

65. WHAT IS NAFTA?

THE NORTH AMERICAN Free Trade Agreement began by joining the two biggest North American economies: Canada and the United States. The goal was simple: remove all barriers to trade between the member countries. With the subsequent addition of Mexico as a full member, NAFTA had combined radically different economies into a single economic zone.

Unlike the European Union (see *What Are Free-Trade Megazones?*), NAFTA is strictly a free-trade agreement—no new tariffs and quotas were imposed on goods coming from outside the free-trade area, and almost all barriers to trade within NAFTA were completely eliminated. Stretching from the cold Arctic tundra to balmy Caribbean shores, NAFTA's goal was simply to allow each country to benefit from the other countries' *comparative advantages.*

Instead of trying to grow tobacco in the Yukon, Canadians found out they would be much better off if they imported these goods from their neighbors to the south, providing other goods and services in return, such as timber or banking. When Wal-Mart set up shopping centers across Mexico, Mexicans found out they could buy well-made American products for a fraction of their previous cost, allowing them to build a more efficient economy and earn extra money exporting Mexican-made products to the north.

In the United States and Canada, the debate over enlarging NAFTA centered mainly on jobs. How could they open their borders to trade, especially to a country with lower labor costs, and not lose jobs at home? The leaders calculated that, in the long term, opening borders to trade would lead to a net increase in jobs as local industries expanded to take advantage of the new trade zone—and they were right. By the end of the 1990s, expanded trade had created many more jobs than those lost by opening up to the new markets.

Although it was hard to convince voters that increased

trade meant increased jobs, the free-trade experiment of NAFTA turned out to be a resounding success. In addition to increasing jobs and economic growth in the United States and Canada, NAFTA succeeded in creating new jobs and businesses in Mexico, helping the country to reduce poverty and the pressure for its citizens to emigrate northward to find jobs.

NAFTA has proven that trade is not a zero-sum game, where one country's gain is another country's loss. Open markets provided an incentive for producers on both sides of the border to concentrate on producing those goods and services where they have a competitive advantage. Canada, for example, saw that it could import appliances made in Mexico for a fraction of the cost it would take to make them in Canada. Of course, this meant job losses in relatively inefficient Canadian factories. But the lost jobs were quickly made up by expanding production of other goods and services, such as auto manufacturing that suddenly had a whole new market "south of the border."

66. WHAT ARE FREE-TRADE MEGAZONES?

INSPIRED BY THE success of the free-trade zones in Europe and North America, during the 1990s many regions of the world moved to build free-trade "megazones" of their own.

In South America, MERCOSUR (Mercado Commún del Sur, or in Brazil, MERCOSUL) joined four countries in a free-trade block in the early 1990s. Brazil and Argentina, two of the biggest economies of the southern hemisphere, were joined by

Paraguay and Uruguay in a common market. Like the European union, MERCOSUR reduced tariffs on trade between the member countries while keeping common tariffs on goods from outside the block.

For the first time, Argentina and Brazil worked together in an economic union and the effects were stupendous: trade soared. Everything from beer and automobiles to fruit and banking services flowed in increasing numbers between the four nations. Soon Chile joined as an associate member. It was only when the Brazilian currency was devalued, following the Asian Crisis in the late 1990s, that trade was interrupted. The suddenly weak Brazilian currency caused enormous distortions—especially in trade with Argentina, which had linked its currency to the dollar (see *What Is Dollarization?*).

Meanwhile, farther to the north, the Andean Pact was formed to remove barriers to trade between Venezuela, Columbia, Peru, Ecuador, and Bolivia. The smaller economies of Central and South America also joined to form two more trading blocks: the Central American Common Market (CACM)—bringing together Guatemala, Costa Rica, El Salvador, Honduras, and Nicaragua; and the Caribbean Community (CARICOM) free-trade zone—including Jamaica, Trinidad & Tobago, and Surinam.

Western Hemisphere leaders have moved to join together all of these disparate groups. At a summit meeting in Miami in 1994, plans were announced to create a "Free Trade Area of the Americas," joining together all of the free-market economies of North, Central, and south America (see *What Is NAFTA?*). A first move in this direction was provided by Chile, which signed free-trade agreements with all three NAFTA members.

The eighteen countries that made up the Asia-Pacific Economic Cooperation Forum also announced the intention of forming a pan-Pacific free-trade area that would include all of the major economies bordering the Pacific, including China and the United States. With almost half of the world's population and most of its cross-border trade, the Pacific-rim free-trade zone, if implemented, would greatly surpass all the other free-trade areas of the world combined.

Faced with expanding trade zones elsewhere, the European Union has also begun to expand to the east and the south (see *What Is the European Union?*). Plans were made to create a Euro-Mediterranean free-trade megazone, giving EU members access to many markets in Northern Africa, including Morocco, Algeria, and Tunisia. This zone was also projected to expand to the eastern Mediterranean, encompassing Israel and several Arab countries in the Middle East. In addition to fostering economic growth, one of the main goals of this new free-trade megazone was to promote political stability—guaranteeing peaceful and secure borders for all of its member states.

67. WHAT ARE THE OECD AND G7/G8?

JUST AS THE United Nations Security Council can be used to solve the world's military and political disputes, many problems arising from global trade and investment can be solved through specialized international organizations.

One of the most active groups in formulating common economic goals is the Organization for Economic Co-Operation and Development (OECD). Besides providing statistics and documents on all aspects of the global economy, the OECD serves as a forum for discussions and coordination of economic policy—such as leading the fight to prevent tax havens from helping money-launderers around the world. The OECD, headquartered in Paris, is made up of virtually all of the advanced industrial economies, including the United States, Canada, Japan, Australia, New Zealand, and most Western European countries.

International economic cooperation can also be encouraged through periodic summits. The granddaddy of these summits is the G7, which becomes the G8, "Group of Eight," whenever Russia joins the meetings. The seven main members— the United States, Canada, Japan, Germany, Italy, Britain, and France—started the meetings as an economic forum, giving the leaders a chance to discuss economic problems in an intimate setting. But the G7 forum has been expanded to cover a wide range of international issues, such as Eastern European economic reform and the protection of the whales. A larger group, called the G20, includes representatives from developing countries as well. Another group, the G77, brings together leaders of developing countries to discuss issues of particular importance to the Third World.

Most world leaders have come to realize that the world's economic problems are, in fact, inseparable from political and military conflicts. Iraq's decision to invade Kuwait, for example, was motivated by access to Kuwait's oil fields and shipping facilities. The rebels in Sierra Leone were driven, in large part, by the prospect of taking over the valuable diamond mines.

The World Bank has estimated that in the forty-seven civil wars that took place during the last forty years of the twentieth century, the single biggest motivating factor was access to commodities like diamonds and drugs. If the importing countries of the world make it clear that plundered goods will find no markets, it will help immeasurably to reduce the incidence of profit-motivated wars throughout the world.

The United Nations also provides several forums for encouraging economic cooperation and evaluating economic growth around the world. One example is the UN Human Development Index, an indicator of longevity, literacy, and standard of living in countries around the world.

The United Nations also has other specialized groups that help economic cooperation, such as the United Nations Development Program (UNDP) and the United Nations Committee on Trade and Development (UNCTAD), which organize high-level conferences that bring rich and poor countries together to confront pressing development issues.

In the end, the resolution of most international issues, such as global pollution, trade imbalances, and access to the sea's resources, will depend on countries working together—often through international groups and agencies such as the United Nations, the G7/G8 summits, and the OECD.

68. WHAT ARE REGIONAL DEVELOPMENT BANKS?

WHEN A NEIGHBORHOOD bank decides to provide low-interest loans to build local homes and businesses, the whole community often benefits from the increased economic activity. In the same way, the world's regional development banks provide funds to encourage growth in poor countries. These development bank loans have become a convenient channel to get funds from rich countries to the "have-nots."

Development banks are not ordinary profit-oriented banks in that they do not take deposits. They are funded by large capital commitments and loans from developed nations such as the United States, Japan, Switzerland, and the European Union. This money is then lent at a low rate of interest to needy countries around the world.

Development bank loans often include a grace period of two to seven years before the borrower has to start paying back the original amount borrowed, the principal. This leeway period provides time for the funded projects—an electric power plant, for example—to start making a profit before the principal payments begin.

The biggest regional development bank is the Inter-American Development Bank (IADB), based in Washington, D.C. Funded primarily by the United States and Canada, the IADB provides loans for development projects throughout the Western Hemisphere. Many countries in Latin America and the Caribbean have seen their infrastructure improved immeasurably after the IADB provided funds for such projects as roads, water supply, and public transport systems.

The Asian Development Bank (ADB) was set up to foster growth in Asia and the Pacific region. Headquartered in the Philippines, the ADB provides most of its loans for agricultural projects in such countries as Indonesia, Pakistan, and Thailand.

Following the decision of the Eastern European countries to move to free-market economies, the European Bank for Reconstruction and Development (EBRD) was set up in London. The EBRD's first priority was financing private sector projects, but only those that local banks were reluctant to get involved in without foreign support, such as loans to help privatize state-owned mines and railways. After beginning its work in the relatively well-off countries of Hungary, Poland, and the Czech Republic, the EBRD embarked on a process of "graduation"—winding down its lending in Central Europe in order to free up funds for the poorer countries further east, such as Romania and Bulgaria.

The EBRD has also become active in ensuring that businesses and banks become more user-friendly. For example, it has launched several lawsuits in Russia to protect shareholders' rights—thus ensuring a stable and transparent environment for future economic growth.

69. WHAT ROLE DO CHARITIES AND NGOS PLAY IN THE WORLD ECONOMY?

NON-GOVERNMENTAL ORGANIZATIONS, or NGOs, are rapidly becoming major players in the world economy. Each year, billions of dollars flow into organizations ranging from the Red Cross and Save the Children to C.A.R.E. and Greenpeace. The money is used primarily for distributing relief in famine-ravaged or war-torn countries.

Other NGOs promote various political, religious, or economic issues that are important to their members. Greenpeace, one of the best-known international NGOs, works in a proactive way, striving to prevent ecological disasters from ever occurring. Amnesty International works in a more reactive way, trying to end repression or unfair imprisonment for such things as political beliefs, sexual orientation, or religious affiliation.

By the year 2000, there were approximately thirty thousand NGOs in the world, most of them small organizations set up in developing countries to help distribute the enormous amount of food and other aid that flows in. Some are huge organizations with multimillion dollar budgets, and many receive money from governments around the world. *Médecins sans Frontières* (Doctors Without Borders), the Nobel Prize–winning organization that provides medical relief to needy countries, gets almost half its income from government sources in the European Union. Oxfam, a British charity combating world hunger, gets a quarter of its money from the British government and the European Union. Sometimes even religious NGOs (also called RINGOs) are asked by donor governments to help distribute goods to troubled spots in the world.

Some NGOs take an active role in politics. Using the motto, "Civil war demands civil action," many NGOs get involved in resolving conflict as well as providing aid. The Carter Center, for example, worked with UNICEF (The United Nations Children and Educational Fund) to broker a peace deal between Uganda and Sudan. *Saint Egidio,* an Italian NGO, played a major role in helping to end the civil war in Mozambique. And Saferworld, another active international NGO, works to restrict arms flow into war-torn areas.

Instead of simply reacting to problems around the world, some NGOs work to prevent problems from arising. The Save the Children Fund, for example, helps villages and families build the necessary infrastructure and educational resources to prevent poverty and famine from occurring. The Red Cross has embarked upon a similar strategy, noting that the number of people dying of infectious diseases in the world—from malaria to tuberculosis to AIDS—was more than a hundred times greater than the total amount of people dying in natural catastrophes such as floods or cyclones. By spending as little as five dollars per person on health care, it was discovered, the lives of millions of people around the world could be saved.

Some charitable groups concentrate on preventing the

exploitation of workers in the world economy. The Fair Labor Association (FLA) is one of the many human-rights groups active on college campuses and elsewhere, working to find a solution to the sweatshop conditions in many factories in developing countries. The goal is to build coalitions of companies, consumers, and social activists to guarantee workers' rights—including freedom of association, minimum wages, maximum working hours, and adequate bathrooms and safety.

Some charities and NGOs are criticized for going too far in working with corrupt government officials, or buying back children sold into slavery, which is criticized by some as only encouraging nefarious behavior. Another criticism is that foreign aid sometimes ends up prolonging wars or is used to support only one side. Such was the case in Ethiopia when the government in control prevented NGOs from distributing needed food to the government's opponents.

Despite the drawback of not having direct government support, many charities and NGOs play a major role in the world economy. Their "comparative advantage" is in being able to deliver aid and effect change without the drawbacks and bureaucracies of traditional politically motivated organizations.

70. HOW IS CORRUPTION PART OF THE WORLD ECONOMY?

FOR BUSINESSES AND governments in many countries around the world, corruption is a way of life. In many countries in Northern Africa, for example, it is necessary to pay government officials a "gratuity" in order to get a passport issued—just like in the movie *Casablanca*. In Europe, business bribes have been common practice for centuries. And in Utah recently, Olympic officials were bribed so they would award the Winter Games to Salt Lake City.

Many government officials who accept payoffs point out that their salaries are extremely low precisely because it is assumed their income will be supplemented by bribes—just as a waiter in New York will accept a lower salary knowing that a large portion of the day's income will come in the form of tips. *Mordida* in Mexico, *baksheesh* in Egypt, *dash* in Kenya—many business deals around the world would be impossible without some sort of supplemental payment. For many international businesspeople, it often seems impossible to compete abroad without getting dirty. Imagine trying to get good service in a restaurant if the waiters know you're not going to give them a tip at the end of the meal.

Undercover payments have reached crisis proportions in some parts of the world. In China and Nigeria, just to name two cases, many free-market reforms have been seriously jeopardized by corrupt business practices—and it is the poor people who suffer the most. It has been estimated that more than $50 billion is illegally transferred from developing countries every year. Most of the money "earned" by corrupt businesspeople and government officials ends up in rich-country banks, far from the lands where it was originally stolen, and where it could be used for desperately needed economic growth.

One way for honest businesspeople to avoid corruption is to have clear laws in their home country specifically forbidding bribery in their business dealings abroad. The United States, for example, prohibits international bribery through the Foreign Corrupt Practices Act. The idea is that once foreigners know that businesspeople are prohibited from providing bribes, they will often not ask for one.

Nonprofit organizations, such as Berlin-based Transparency International (TI), fight graft by calling for greater visibility in all international business transactions. TI has also worked closely with the Paris-based Organization for Economic Cooperation and Development (OECD) to fight international corruption by agreeing on a convention, to be signed by all the major economic powers, which specifically prohibits the practice of bribing foreign public officials while conducting international business transactions.

The Internet also helps immeasurably in fighting corruption. The fact that more and more business is being done over the Web with business dealings online and in full view of everyone leaves fewer opportunities for corruption and shady deals in the world economy.

71. WHAT IS MONEY LAUNDERING?

EVERY ONCE IN a while, the world's criminals need to recycle their "dirty money" in order to wash away any traces of its illegal past. A Spanish drug dealer, for example, may end a day's work with a large amount of cash that needs to be deposited or otherwise spent.

Since there's a limit to the number of Miami condominiums or luxury automobiles a drug dealer can pay cash for without creating suspicion, illicit earnings somehow have to be put into a bank.

The idea of any money-laundering scheme is to get illegally earned money into legitimate bank accounts without alerting anyone to the money's past. The best way to do this is to transfer the money from another "respectable" bank account. But it all has to start somewhere. One popular money-laundering practice is to make hundreds of small deposits into a bank account rather than a single large deposit, which would normally be reported to law-enforcement agencies. This can be done best by mixing the money with legal deposits—using a restaurant's bank account, for instance, preferably one with a lot of cash deposits.

Once money is in a legitimate bank account, it can be transferred around the world quite easily without interference from the authorities. This is possible because most international bank transfers are simply electronic messages sent from one bank to another. A bank in Miami could transfer money to London by using a correspondent bank that would simply credit the account of one bank and debit the account of another. The sheer size of these international transfers—more than one trillion dollars a day by some estimates—makes it difficult to control money laundering. The illegal transfers simply disappear into a sea of legal ones.

Another way to get illegal money into the banking system is to first put the money in a bank that asks few questions about the money's origin. Since the early 1990s several countries, such as Switzerland, have restricted money coming from unknown sources. Others, such as those in tax havens in the Caribbean, are notorious for being easy on money launderers, asking few questions about the money's origin. Once a bank in the Cayman Islands or Aruba sends the money to a respectable bank, it is usually too late to track the money's source. Money launderers also use several different bank transfers to get the money into the bank where they actually use it, by which time no one has any idea where it originated.

Several international groups—such as the Financial Stability Forum (FSF), the Financial Action Task Force (FATF), and the OECD (see *What Are the OECD and G7/G8?*)—have made efforts to investigate the money-laundering activities of various countries around the world. They have even gone so far as to list the countries that are seen as being lax or uncooperative in dealing with the problem. A list published by the Financial Stability Forum in the year 2000, named the following countries: Anguilla, Antigua and Barbuda, Aruba, Belize, British Virgin Islands, Cayman Islands, Cook Islands, Costa Rica, Cyprus, Lebanon, Liechtenstein, Marshall Islands, Mauritius, Nauru, Netherlands Antilles, Niue, Panama, St. Kitts and Nevis, St. Lucia, St. Vincent and the Grenadines, Samoa, Seychelles, the Bahamas, Turks and Caicos, and Vanuatu. Those countries placed in an "intermediate" category include: Andorra, Bahrain, Macau, Malta, and Monaco.

What can be done? Some countries in the European Union have threatened to ban all transactions with banks that are known to encourage or turn a blind eye to money laundering. Others have proposed making international loans and aid contingent on honest banking standards. The amount of illegal money that gets discovered, however, is just the tip of the iceberg. Global money laundering, it is estimated, moves anywhere from a half a trillion to 1.5 trillion dollars per year—more than the entire economic output of most countries.

The currency of choice for most money launderers is the U.S. dollar. This partly explains why more than half the "greenbacks" printed cannot be found anywhere in the U.S. economy. Drug lords in Latin America, prostitutes in Southeast Asia, and Russian "Mafiosi" all make heavy use of the U.S. dollar for their illegal activities, which is why laundering U.S. dollars is easier than laundering other currencies. The dollar is especially prized for its "liquidity" in the sense that it can be exchanged almost anywhere in the world without raising suspicion.

72. HOW DOES A SWISS BANK ACCOUNT WORK?

SWITZERLAND IS ONE of the few countries in the world that guarantees, by law, the secrecy of its bank accounts. As long as the client of a Swiss bank has not done anything considered illegal in Switzerland, the bank cannot reveal the client's identity to anyone, under penalty of law. Switzerland, therefore, has often been seen as a financial haven in a turbulent world. During the two World Wars, for example, many families from war-torn France, Italy, Germany, and Austria were able to keep their savings secure in a Swiss bank.

The manner in which the Swiss handled the accounts that went unclaimed after World War II became a major international scandal in the late 1990s. It was revealed that family members—many of them children of Holocaust victims—were told they had to provide exhaustive documentation in order to get access to accounts that rightly belonged to them. Only after intense international pressure did the Swiss banks reveal how many of these "sleeping" accounts existed—thousands, in fact. The Swiss banks made a multibillion dollar settlement with Holocaust survivors and their representatives to make up for their failure to help most of these *dormant account* holders recover their families' lost fortunes.

Opening a numbered, "secret" Swiss bank account is still relatively easy to do—usually involving nothing more than going to Switzerland and filling out an account opening form, making a deposit, and declaring who the owner of the money really is. After a wave of international pressure to stop money laundering, all holders of Swiss bank accounts are now required to declare the "beneficial owner" and provide a plausible explanation for where the money came from (see *What Is Money Laundering?*). In addition, Swiss fund managers are now required by law to report suspected money laundering to the authorities. This is not the case in most countries.

Money launderers often prefer Swiss bank accounts to hide their ill-gotten gains because once money passes through a respectable Swiss bank, it is accepted anywhere in the world. Many criminals in the world economy, from Russian black marketeers to Third World dictators, have used Swiss banks for this reason. However, most people holding Swiss bank accounts do not use them to launder illegally earned money. They merely want their legally earned funds to be safe and free from government control and taxes at home. Citizens from turbulent or high-tax economies—in Latin America, for example—count on the Swiss reputation for honesty and discretion to preserve their capital for the generations to come.

Since tax evasion is not considered "illegal" in Switzerland—it is only a civil, not a criminal offense—earnings in Swiss bank accounts remain a secret from the authorities in the client's home country. Essentially, foreigners with legally earned money can keep their funds in Swiss bank accounts without fear of ever being reported to their home countries, as long as they break no Swiss laws.

In the year 2000, the European Union established a system to require all countries in Europe—even those that are not EU members, such as Switzerland—to provide the names of Euro-

pean tax evaders to their home governments. If the Swiss decide
to go along, it will involve yet another major change to the cherished concept of Swiss banking secrecy.

73. WHAT ARE TAX HAVENS?

THE TERM TAX haven usually conjures up images of
palm trees and shady criminals sitting around swimming
pools drinking banana daiquiris.

The main purpose of a tax haven is not to facilitate illegal
international activities, but to attract business to otherwise over-
looked economic centers by reducing or eliminating taxes completely. The most popular tax havens are found on islands in the
Caribbean, such as the Netherlands Antilles or the British Virgin
Islands. Tax havens can also be found in the Pacific—Vanuatu
and Samoa are two examples—or in such Central American
countries as Panama and Costa Rica. In Europe, many small
city-states, such as Andorra or Monaco, have been transformed
into lucrative tax havens. The British writer Somerset Maugham
once described Monaco as a "sunny place for shady people."

Many tax havens, such as the Cayman Islands or the UK's
Isle of Man, require little or no taxes from companies domiciled
there. This is a lucrative opportunity that many businesses and
individuals just cannot pass up. Just as many U.S. companies
choose to register their headquarters in Delaware to take advantage of lower taxes and favorable laws, many international
companies set up subsidiaries in international tax havens such as
Liechtenstein or Panama. The United States, for example, has

explicitly allowed U.S. exporters to set up shell companies abroad to avoid paying U.S. taxes on their exports.

Tax havens end up being the perfect place for companies to book their profits. A Brazilian company exporting coffee, for example, may set up an offshore company in the British Virgin Islands and take advantage of the offshore company's tax-free status by selling the coffee to the BVI company at an artificially low price and then immediately reselling the coffee to companies in Europe at the higher market level. This allows the exporter to pocket the profits offshore where there are no taxes. The home country government may feel cheated out of its legitimate tax on the real profit, but because a tax haven was used as a go-between, the money that would normally be paid as tax ends up in the pockets of the exporter.

Many individuals also set up their "domicile" in tax havens such as the Bahamas or Cayman Islands. Just as a company avoids taxes on profits in these havens, individuals avoid paying taxes on income. It is mainly for this reason that tax havens flourish. The Cayman Islands, for example, has become the fifth-largest banking center in the world, with approximately six hundred banks and trust companies managing assets exceeding a half trillion dollars.

Tax havens are also becoming domiciles-of-choice for many Web-based companies. The idea is to avoid government regulation of cyberspace, in much the same way as companies move to tax havens to avoid government taxes. If Napster, for example, had been domiciled in the UK island of Jersey or on one of the offshore oil platforms that are being set up to allow companies to avoiding government regulation of cyberspace activities—it would never have had to bow to record company demands to pay royalties to Web-based transfers of music.

Many developed country governments are worried that

tax havens are becoming centers for money-laundering and other illegal activities (see *What Is Money Laundering?*). Just as globalization has made it easier to move capital around the world, it has also made it easier to hide illegal money—and tax havens provide a perfect place to do it. The illegal money often gets covered up by the billions of dollars that are flowing through tax haven banks on any given day of the year.

74. HOW ARE ILLEGAL GOODS TRADED ON THE WORLD'S BLACK MARKETS?

ENORMOUS AMOUNTS OF illegal or semi-legal goods and services—ranging from elephant tusks to Ecstasy—are traded daily on the world's black markets.

Drugs are by far the most commonly traded good on the world's black markets. More than sixty billion dollars of illegal drugs are sold every year—from the back streets of Milan to dorm rooms in Ohio. With the amount of trade in illegal drugs surpassing the total economic output of most Third World countries, it is hard to discourage the trade in lucrative cash crops such as heroin and coca. Poor farmers in Peru, for example, find it difficult to switch back to vegetables once they have begun growing coca.

Some progress is being made, however, by offering economic incentives, such as better schools and access to government support for community development programs. Eliminating drug production in selected areas, however, is a bit like squeezing a balloon. Pushing in one or two places just makes other parts expand. After coca production in Peru and Bolivia was reduced in the late 1990s, for example, the loss in production was quickly replaced by expanded production in Colombia and other Andean countries. In the end, there was no significant change on the world markets. The price of cocaine in the United States and Europe was no higher than before the billions of dollars were spent eradicating its production.

Many leaders point out that drugs, like alcohol, will always be a part of society and that it is a waste of resources to try to eliminate their production. Others say that instead of trying to suppress the supply, more efforts should be made to reduce the demand through more education or stricter enforcement of drug laws in the countries where they are consumed.

Demand-side solutions can also be applied to other products traded on the world's black markets, such as endangered animal parts. Making it illegal to sell ivory from elephant tusks on the international markets certainly helped to stop the slaughter of elephants in many African countries, but progress was mitigated by the fact that the price for ivory on the world's black markets rose dramatically—providing even more incentive for poachers to kill elephants. In response, some environmental groups decided to try to experiment with a controlled sale of ivory, allowing legally harvested ivory—from over-populated elephant herds, for example—to be sold in carefully controlled ways.

The Convention on International Trade in Endangered Species (CITES) along with the United Nations Environment Program (UNEP) have often worked together to regulate the trade in endangered species of wild fauna and flora. By controlling the sale of ivory poaching has been reduced to a minimum.

Another, more gruesome product traded on the world's black markets are human organs. In Malaysia, where the average wait for a new kidney is sixteen years, many patients travel to China where they are able to buy kidneys, often from executed criminals. It is estimated that more than a thousand Malaysians have kidneys they bought on the black market, usually by paying bribes to doctors or prison officials in China. The Transplantation Society, a leading international medical forum based in Montreal, has banned the use of organs from executed criminals, calling the practice barbaric. But as long as there are patients whose only other alternative is a life tied to a dialysis machine, the illicit trade in body parts will certainly continue.

Diamonds and other precious commodities also find their way onto black markets, especially during times of war. In Sierra Leone, for example, the rebels fighting against government and UN forces started mining diamonds to pay for guns and other war material. It was even suspected that the war was not about ethnic or tribal conflicts at all, but rather about access to the riches in the local diamond mines. The UN Security Council declared an embargo, banning the sale of diamonds from Sierra Leone on the world markets. But the difficulty of identifying these "illegal" diamonds meant that many were able to end up being traded on black markets—and subsequently in respectable jewelry shops around the world.

Other black market trading includes: rare birds, whale meat, rare tropical woods, and rhinoceros horns, which are ground up and sold as male potency medications. Even legal drugs, such as those for AIDS and tuberculosis that are distributed at reduced cost in one country, often end up being sold on black markets in other parts of the world.

The best solution for most black market abuses is concerted consumer efforts on a global level. If every country in the world refused to import illegal products, including products made with slave labor, the production and sale of these goods could be greatly reduced. Some consumer groups recommend the use of certificates on goods attesting to their legal origin. By working with countries that have been less than vigilant in the past, the other countries of the world can use their economic leverage to end much of the world's black market activity.

75. WHAT IS ECONOMIC ESPIONAGE?

WITH THE END of the Cold War, most people thought spying would become a relic of the past. The world was shocked in the late 1990s, however, when an outraged European Parliament began investigating the Anglo-American electronic spy network called "echelon," charging that it was being used for economic espionage between putative allies.

The echelon system is run by the U.S. National Security Agency and consists of a vast combination of spy satellites and sensitive listening stations scattered across the globe that are able to eavesdrop on virtually every electronic communication crossing a national border. It was set up as a joint venture between Britain and the United States to intercept radio, telephone, and telex transmissions. Listening stations can be found in virtually every English-speaking country, from Australia to England to Canada to New Zealand.

Although echelon's original purpose was to help Western governments keep abreast of covert enemy activity during the cold war, it was long suspected of being used to monitor communications between allies as well. When a German government minister accused the British of using the system to get "priority information" on German and French companies, the controversy was finally out in the open.

What makes echelon so effective is its use of supercomputers to filter phone calls or other forms of communications, searching for trigger words that may lead to uncovering a terrorist plot—although the information can just as easily be used for economic espionage. Speech recognition programs and text-search programs sift through the mounds of information and when certain target words are found, the intercept is handed over to humans to analyze. If a phone call travels by satellite or microwave at any time during its journey, which most do, it is almost certainly picked up by echelon.

Not only can the system monitor satellite broadcasts of telephone or Internet messages, it can also tap undersea cables as well as microwave tower networks. Because of the growing use of faxes, e-mail, and other forms of Internet communication, deciphering communication is becoming much easier—computers can manipulate digital information much more easily than normal speech.

A parallel system has been developed by the FBI to wiretap the Internet. The system, dubbed "Carnivore" because of its ability to find the meat in any e-mail sent anywhere in the world, uses high technology computer-aided search tools to assemble the different parts of each message sent over the Internet. Many civil libertarians have criticized this and other surveillance systems as unlawful intrusions on citizens' private correspondence.

As the amount of information that is sent over the airwaves increases, it is only a matter of time before some of the information is used for economic espionage. Canadian spies have been caught using spy satellites to pick up information on a U.S.-China grain deal, for example. This information was then used to help Canadian companies bidding for the same business.

Another case involved Boeing, which was accused by the Europeans of using economic espionage to learn about impending deals of its rival, Airbus.

The response from some government officials is that they do, in fact, spy on companies, but only to uncover cases of industrial bribery, which is illegal in most—but unfortunately not all—advanced industrial economies. The "we *have* spied on you, but only because you bribe" response angers many countries because they consider the use of spy satellites for industrial espionage a clear breach of trust.

The question of economic espionage is made even more complicated by the increasingly interconnected world economy. Given the choice, which company should a U.S. spy system help first: an IBM subsidiary in Germany or a Mercedes Benz factory in Alabama? Long time military and political alliances, like everything else in the New Economy, are slowly becoming obsolete.

76. HOW IS THE ENVIRONMENT AFFECTED BY THE WORLD ECONOMY?

IT IS NOT always obvious, but every one of the world's manmade environmental problems is the direct result of an economic decision. Industrial pollution exists because it is more expensive to clean up pollutants than it is to dump them into the water and into the air. No one wants to pollute, but environmental protection, like all other economic decisions, involves an economic tradeoff. Companies, countries, and even consumers must decide how much they are ready to pay to keep the environment clean and healthy. This decision is, essentially, an economic one.

Industrial nations have often treated many of the world's resources as if they were disposable commodities. This ignores a basic economic concept: all factors of production—whether land, labor, or clean water—are *scarce* commodities and have a price that should be factored into every business decision. Clean air and water, for example, were once thought of as limitless. In fact, they have been rapidly "depleted," to use an economic term, by burgeoning populations and rampant industrial development. This is occurring around the world, in the rich countries as well as in the poor. Basically, there are two ways to get consumers and businesses to reduce environmentally harmful activity. One is the "stick" of economic sanctions; the other is the "carrot" of economic incentives.

Economic sanctions are often the most effective way to change environmentally unsound practices and policies. When a company is forced to pay for its pollution, it will think twice before discharging waste into the air and into the water. If a government were forced to include the depletion of natural resources in its calculation of economic activity—creating an "environmental GDP," for example—it would have a vast effect on public policy.

Making consumers pay for natural resources, such as water and air, can have a profound effect on conservation. Most of the world's fresh water, for example, is currently wasted because most homes and businesses have no economic incentive to conserve. In most countries water is not metered and government subsidies encourage water wastage in industry and farming.

One solution is to allow private companies to install water systems and charge people for the amount of water they use.

This provides a constant supply of water at rates that are almost always less than the cost of bringing it in by truck. In the Ivory Coast, after the water supply was given to a private company to manage, Abidjan became one of the few large African cities with a reliable, relatively inexpensive water supply.

Some criticize these privatization plans, fearing that the poorest people will be made victims of rampant capitalist greed. The opposite has often been the case, however. In Buenos Aires, for example, when a French water company was allowed to buy a share of the local water system in the late 1990s, the reach of the system was extended to many poor outlying areas of the capital without any increase in rates.

Economic incentives can also be effective in protecting the environment. After years of seeing vast swaths of the Amazon rain forest destroyed by rampant burning by farmers, an international program was set up to promote environmentally friendly economic development. This plan called for a combination of eco-tourism, more responsible wood-cutting (such as only cutting down specific types of trees), and, above all, economic incentives to keep the forests alive. One plan encouraged local people to go into the forests to pick guaraná berries, a natural stimulant used in popular soft drinks. Harvesting the fruit of trees, and not the trees themselves, would ensure that the forests were kept alive for future generations, and, in addition, provide thousands of jobs to local inhabitants. Once it is shown that precious wildlife and trees are worth more alive than dead, people begin to change their environmentally—and economically—destructive behavior.

In the end, a healthy environment is not necessarily incompatible with a prosperous economy. Indeed, some of the world's worst pollution has occurred in poor countries, such as those in the former Soviet bloc in Eastern Europe. The nuclear tragedy of Chernobyl and the destruction of the Aral Sea are just two examples. In fact, some of the world's cleanest air and water can be found in the richest, most advanced industrial economies— such as Sweden, Denmark, and Canada.

By looking at environmental issues from a global perspective, it becomes clear that protecting the environment is not only good for human health, but will also allow the world to sustain healthy economic growth in the years to come.

77. HOW CAN ECONOMIC INCENTIVES BE USED TO REDUCE POLLUTION?

ONE OF THE most difficult problems facing the world economy is how to provide jobs and a higher standard of living for the world's growing population without destroying the environment.

One solution, as strange as it may sound, is for countries and businesses to sell "pollution rights" to one another. Many environmental groups have come to support such programs because they come as close as possible to solving two seemingly irreconcilable goals: economic growth and a clean environment.

Fortunately, there is quite an efficient way of separating the "good" from the "bad" polluters: the invisible hand of the marketplace. There is really no such thing as a good polluter, but those that produce needed goods for an economy in an efficient way should not suffer the same restrictions on pollution as the others. How does it work? The key to pollution rights plans, also called "emission rights" plans, is to induce companies and other polluters to decrease their output of harmful emissions in the most efficient way possible.

The problem of previous anti-pollution campaigns was that governments, in effect, gave everyone the right to pollute, regardless of how useful they were to the economy at large. However, under a "pollution rights" plan, governments recognize that there are vast differences between polluters in any given economy: some should be allowed to grow and provide jobs and products for the economy, while others should be encouraged to go out of business. This can be done by putting a "cost" on pollution.

An efficiently run wheelchair factory, for example, often produces much less pollution per wheelchair than an inefficient one. Under traditional anti-pollution plans, the government would have reduced production at both plants. But under a pollution rights plan, the efficient wheelchair producer could "buy" pollution rights from the inefficient one and use those rights to produce many more wheelchairs for a given amount of pollution—making everyone in the economy better off with no increase in pollution.

Road pricing works in a similar way, providing economic incentives to drivers to reduce their polluting activity. Supported by the Sierra Club and other environmental groups, road pricing consists of charging different prices for road use, according to the time of day and the pollution levels. By charging more to use the road at rush hour, for example, road pricing reduces delays and, in the end, reduces pollution.

In San Diego, the price for using the special lanes is flashed on screens along the roadway, usually half a mile before the lanes start. Drivers can choose whether they want to use the lanes at that price, pull off and use another route, or abandon using a car altogether. Making people pay extra for the right to pollute often leads to significant reduction of their environmentally harmful economic behavior. In San Diego, cars that use the special lanes are charged per mile by an electronic "transponder" installed in the roadbed.

A similar system is being implemented in London. Basically, road pricing imposes the cost of roads and pollution on the people who drive the most. It is similar to putting tolls on bridges to pay for their construction and upkeep, but road pricing goes further to discourage drivers from using their polluting cars, trucks, and sport utility vehicles at specific times during the day. This powerful economic incentive forces commuters to make more efficient use of roads, or even switch to less expensive—and less polluting—ways to get to work, such as carpools or public transportation.

78. HOW DOES IMMIGRATION AFFECT THE WORLD ECONOMY?

A DEMOGRAPHIC TIME bomb is ticking in the world economy. Citizens in wealthy countries are not having enough babies—and they are living longer, creating an acute shortage of labor in most advanced industrial economies. Meanwhile, populations are exploding in many other parts of the world.

It is estimated that the United States needs to bring in more than ten million immigrants per year just to keep the ratio of workers to retired people steady. The European Union will need more than a million immigrants a year just to keep its working age population stable between now and the year 2050, and in Japan the ratio of retired people to workers is expected to double in twenty years. Who will take care of all those retirees?

One answer is to increase immigration. Contrary to popular belief, in most countries, legal immigrants rarely go on welfare and their children are usually among the most motivated students at school. In the U.S. high-tech industry, for example, immigrants provide 30 percent of the manpower and 20 percent of the managerial talent. In England, Indian restaurants employ more people than the entire British steel industry—and many of those employees are immigrants.

Unskilled immigrants also help the economy by doing the jobs most people in wealthy industrial countries refuse to do. An eighteen-year-old British college student may not think it is "trendy" to work in an old age home, but for someone from India, going to London to work, even in a retirement home, could be a dream come true.

Without immigrants, the U.S. growth rate in the late 1990s would certainly have led to acute labor shortages, rising inflation, and an overheating economy. Nevertheless, many people, especially labor unions, oppose immigration, saying that immigrants depress the wages. A German plan to import software programmers from India brought cries of *"Kinder statt Inder"* (children instead of Indians), implying that the lack of skilled workers should be solved by training the young. Paradoxically, the countries with the lowest birth rates—Austria, Italy, Germany, and Japan, for example—are sometimes the ones protesting legal immigration the most. The fact is that immigrants often provide the skills and manpower necessary to make the economy stronger, meaning, in the end, still higher wages for everyone.

Illegal immigration poses even greater problems. When fifty-eight Chinese people hidden in a tomato cargo truck were found dead after crossing the English Channel, a whole different side of immigration was exposed: the large-scale trafficking of human beings.

It has been estimated that more than thirty million people are smuggled across international borders each year, bringing the smugglers billions of dollars in revenue. Sometimes whole villages pay to have family members smuggled into wealthy countries abroad, expecting to be repaid ten-fold when the money starts flowing in from lucrative jobs in rich countries. Many of these immigrants end up working as prostitutes or "soldiers" for illegal gangs. It can take several years to pay off the debt owed to smugglers for getting illegal immigrants into rich countries. The smuggling of human beings has become a form of slavery—except in this case the "slave-traders" are paid by the victims themselves.

Unlike migrations of the past, when hordes of people crossed borders en masse, modern illegal migration usually occurs clandestinely. People cross borders—such as the Rio Grande between Mexico and the United States—in the dark of night or use modern modes of transport such as ships, planes, or even the backs of produce trucks. According to the International Organization for Migration (IOM), the Geneva-based intergovernmental agency that keeps track of international immigration, there are from twenty to forty million "irregular" immigrants in the rich countries of the world, and the problem is getting worse.

As long as huge disparities in wealth exist in the world—and as long as hunger and poverty are allowed to exist in the Third World—immigration, legal or otherwise, will be part of the world economy.

79. HOW ARE SLAVERY AND CHILD LABOR PART OF THE WORLD ECONOMY?

ONE OF THE dirty little secrets of the world economy is that some employees do not have the freedom to leave their jobs. Slavery, although officially illegal, is tolerated in different forms in almost every part of the world, including many advanced industrial economies.

In some countries in Southeast Asia, for example, children are sold into slavery by impoverished parents in the countryside who are paid a generous fee by "employment agents"—who tell the parents that the children will be taken to the big city to find jobs in factories or as "waitresses," which more often than not means working in the sex industry. In India, boys are "sold" by their parents to work in the rug industry. The parents are, again, paid a fee by employment agents—and, in many cases, the boys are forced to work many years in miserable conditions to pay it off.

Basically, there are two kinds of modern-day slavery: *forced labor* and *debt enslavement*.

Forced labor may involve anything from prison labor in China to classic slavery in Southern Sudan, where slave traders literally kidnap young men and women—exactly as slave traders did centuries ago—and force them to work for their new masters, sometimes for the rest of their lives. Some charitable organizations have gone so far as to buy back these slaves and return them to their families, but these practices have been strongly criticized by the United Nations and other non-governmental organizations (see *What Role Do Charities and NGOs Play in the World Economy?*) as an encouragement for modern-day slave traders to continue their nefarious practices.

Another form of forced labor is the practice of enticing people to leave their families, using the pretext of a job as a domestic servant in a neighboring country. Once they get across the border, the victims are sold as virtual slaves, usually to the sex industry. This "sexual servitude" usually ends only when the sex workers have gotten too old or when they contract AIDS or other sexually transmitted diseases. By then, it is often too late: many cannot go home because they would face ostracism for "dishonoring" their families, or because their families were the ones who sold them into servitude in the first place.

Another form of slavery, debt enslavement, exists in almost every country in the world. In the United States, for example, some agricultural workers are hired "for the season" and are then allowed to make purchases on credit at the company store. Often, these purchases consist of nonessential goods such as cigarettes and liquor at highly inflated prices. By the end of the season, workers may end up owing more to the company than they have been paid. Essentially, they end up "owing their souls to the company store." Employees are usually not allowed to leave their jobs—under the threat of physical force—until their debts are paid off.

What can consumers do to stop the practice of slavery and child labor in the world economy? Organizing consumer boycotts of products made by forced labor can be quite effective. In India, for example, the use of child labor in the rug industry or in the making of soccer balls has been reduced drastically after boycotts from consumers in other parts of the world, and many rugs coming from India and Nepal now have tags certifying that they have not been made by children or by forced labor (see www.rugmark.org).

Like many problems in the world economy, the use of child labor is not easily remedied. In most agricultural societies, children are often used to help the family plant and harvest crops—usually involving no real harm to their health or educational growth. In some ways, this is not so different from the practice of children having summer jobs in rich countries. Many international children's aid organizations, therefore, make a distinction between "child labor" and "child work," pointing out that some work—as long as it does not interfere with their schooling—allows many children to earn income and develop skills and self-confidence.

Essentially, all workers in the world economy should have the opportunity to do a job that does not compromise their health or well-being. If a child or an adult worker is forced to work under conditions indistinguishable from slavery, it is up to consumers, governments, and aid organizations around the world to stop the offending practices—using economic or any other force at their disposal.

80. WHAT IS THE EFFECT OF THE AIDS EPIDEMIC ON THE WORLD ECONOMY?

IN ADDITION TO the vast human suffering caused by the worldwide AIDS epidemic, the economies of many countries around the world are being devastated by this disease that shows no signs of abating.

By the year 2000, more than twenty countries in Africa had HIV infection rates above seven percent. In some countries, such as Botswana and Zimbabwe, more than 30 percent of adults were infected and average life expectancy had declined dramatically as adults began dying in large numbers—leaving behind millions of orphaned children. In several Asian countries, waves of new infections have also grown to crisis proportions.

Whole economies around the world are imploding because there is simply no one left to do the work. Because AIDS weakens and kills adults in the prime of their working years, in many countries where AIDS is prevalent there are simply not enough working adults to make the economy function properly. Not only are the main wage earners in many families missing, but spouses and other family members are increasingly required to take time off from work to take care of children left behind when one of the parents dies of AIDS. And when both parents die, many children drop out of school to help out at home. This keeps them from learning the basic skills needed to become productive members of society when they become adults—assuming they live that long. Before AIDS, one in fifty children in poor countries was an orphan. In some countries in Africa, the rate is now one in ten.

According to the World Bank, only 15 percent of Africans live in an environment that it considers adequate for sustainable growth and development, and almost half live in complete poverty. In order to reduce the number of poor people, those economies need annual growth rates of 7 percent or more. Because of AIDS, many economies are only growing at marginal rates, if at all. When 8 percent of adults are infected, per capita growth is 0.4 percent lower than it would have been. When 25 percent are infected, at least 1 percent per year is lost. In many countries, where per capita growth is normally about 1 percent per year, the economic consequences of the AIDS epidemic are mind-boggling.

What about a vaccine? A doctor at the World Health Organization once said that if, by some miracle, it were discovered that clean water would cure AIDS, one-third of the people in the world could still not afford it. A promising solution is the International AIDS Vaccine Initiative, which receives funding from foundations and governments. The group invests the money in individual AIDS researchers and instead of asking for a share of the future revenues, it makes the company agree to distribute the vaccine cheaply in poor countries—assuming a vaccine is discovered.

Until a vaccine is developed, treatment is the only option. But the extreme poverty of many AIDS-stricken countries precludes hope of ever affording the kind of treatment taken for granted in developed countries. In some countries, one year of treatment costs more than an entire family earns. In addition, corruption, inefficient distribution, and greed have distorted the market, making the price of AIDS medication much higher than it should be.

Major drug companies, after a worldwide uproar over profiting from the AIDS crisis in poor developing countries, agreed to provide AIDS drugs "at cost," charging no more than the cost of production for drugs sold in poor countries. Even then, most AIDS drugs are out of reach for most citizens in the world's poorest nations. And without an infrastructure to oversee the proper distribution and use of AIDS medication, not much benefit can be derived from them. In some cases, unsupervised distribution of AIDS medications actually can contribute to the problem by allowing new strains of the disease to develop and spread to other parts of the world.

In an attempt to give many AIDS-stricken countries the possibility to grow their way out of poverty, in the year 2000 the U.S. government passed a law to ease or abolish trade restrictions for forty-eight African countries. But without a productive work force, many countries in Africa find themselves with little to export. The solution, like the disease, is not just a public health issue. It involves a wide range of political, social, and economic aspects.

81. WHAT ARE ECONOMIC SANCTIONS?

HUMAN RIGHTS ABUSES, endangered mountain gorillas, child labor, vanishing trees in the Amazon, slavery, torture, and war. Many illegal practices in the world economy can be altered through economic sanctions—although the final result is sometimes far from ideal.

Basically, there are two kinds of economic sanctions: consumer boycotts and trade embargoes. *Consumer boycotts* can take many forms. Individual consumers making the decision on their own to stop buying products from offending producers can be effective, but only marginally. The loss of one sale is not going to make a company change its practices overnight, but the threat of a wide consumer boycott can be an effective tool. It involves the most powerful economic incentive around: profits. By refusing to buy tuna that came from drift-net fishing, for example, consumers were able to end a practice that had been killing thousands of dolphins per year.

Many organizations now provide consumers with information on which products to buy or not to buy in order to bring about a desired change in the world. The Forest Stewardship Council (FSC), for example, was set up by the WWF to provide consumers with a "seal of approval" that showed that the wood used in the product was harvested using sustainable growth methods. Instead of clear-cutting forests, FSC-approved timber companies only cut selected trees, preserving forests around the world for future generations.

Trade embargoes are usually organized by governments or governmental organizations such as the United Nations to force a country to change harmful or illegal behavior. Although trade embargoes are of dubious economic value, they are sometimes highly effective in bringing about political or social change. The refusal of countries to trade and do business with South Africa, for example, was instrumental in leading to the dismantling of apartheid. But most trade blockades are only marginally effective in forcing countries to change policies that violate human rights or international treaties. Cuba, despite a complete U.S. trade embargo, steadfastly refused to change its communist system of government.

The key with any economic sanction is to have a "critical mass" of support. If only one or two countries refuses to buy fish from countries that kill endangered species of whales, they are unlikely to end their destructive practices. Even when the whole world is behind economic sanctions, they can sometimes backfire. In Iraq, for example, despite UN sponsored economic sanctions, Saddam Hussein was able to consolidate power and even profit from the black markets that emerged after the sanctions were imposed.

In many cases, sanctions help dictators or despots rally their citizens against a common "enemy." During the 1990s, the UN Security Council introduced more sanctions than ever before, but most often they did little good. The offending countries, from Sudan to Iraq, just bunkered down and waited until the trouble blew over.

Unilateral economic sanctions are also of minimal value in getting a country to change its behavior. When the United States imposed a trade embargo on Iran, for example, it ended up damaging American businesses and did little to change Iranian government policies. Without a common front, trade sanctions usually only hurt the country imposing them: French oil companies simply moved in and signed lucrative contracts in Iran when the U.S. pulled out.

Trade restrictions also may end up provoking the targeted country into erecting trade barriers of its own, ultimately hurting consumers and businesses on both sides. When many nations band together to send a clear message, however, threats of retaliation often lose their punch. Trade sanctions agreed to at the United Nations, for example, are much more effective because they are voted on by all the member countries. Although these resolutions are usually non-binding, enforcement is often not necessary if broad support is obtained beforehand.

GLOSSARY

What is a stock option? What exactly is the WTO? What is a derivative? What is the G7? When these terms come up in the course of our daily lives, we sometimes need to refresh our memories. Business meetings, newspapers, Web pages, and TV and radio programs are increasingly referring to events occurring in the world economy. If we are going to be effective players in the World Economy, we need to be able to speak the language.

American Depository Receipt (ADR). ADRs make it easier for North American investors to buy shares of a foreign company. Banks create them by placing shares of a foreign company on deposit in the United States and then issue ADRs that are bought and sold on U.S. exchanges just like the original stock.

Arbitrage. Gives new meaning to the expression "it pays to shop around." An arbitrageur spots discrepancies in world markets, then acts quickly, buying things cheaply in one market and selling them for a profit in another where the prices are higher.

Asset. On a balance sheet, assets are positives. Liabilities are negatives. The assets of most companies include financial assets such as cash and securities, fixed assets such as buildings and computers, and intangible assets such as goodwill.

Asset Stripping. Sometimes, two plus two is more than four. When an undervalued company is acquired, its assets can be sold off to make more money than it took to acquire the company in the first place. Asset stripping is a key factor in the takeover game, where the proceeds from asset sales are often used to pay off the huge amounts of debt incurred to acquire the company.

B2B. Business to business transactions on the Web. The B2B marketplace really took off when companies set up online exchanges to buy materials and other products from each other. These *eHubs* or *eMarketplaces* provide an almost unlimited world of trading partners, leading to significantly lower prices for parts and supplies—and consequently increased productivity for the businesses that use them.

B2C. Business to consumer transactions on the Web. Online retailers provide consumers with a myriad of products and services on the Web. The low cost of doing Web-based business—a new insurance policy online, for example, costs less than a dollar to process—brings enormous economies of scale: prices on the Web are usually much lower than those at normal "bricks-and-mortar" businesses.

Balance of Payments. The sum of a country's international trade is called its balance of payments. This measure includes all of the country's trade in goods, services, and money. It is called a balance because transfers of goods and services abroad are always compensated by transfers of money flowing in the opposite direction. This measure is not to be confused with "Balance of Trade" (see **Merchandise Trade Balance**), which only measures the trade in goods—not services.

Balance Sheet. The snapshot of a company's total assets and liabilities. A balance sheet looks at a company's assets and liabilities at a certain point in time. When the company has more assets than debts on the balance sheet, the stockholders are happy. The difference between the two, called shareholders' equity (see **Stockholders' Equity**), belongs to them.

Bankruptcy. A company that can't pay its debts is said to be "bankrupt." The term has its origins in medieval Italy, where traders who could not pay their bills had their benches broken—*banca rotta* in Italian—to keep them from doing business. In some countries, bankrupt companies are given an opportunity to try to pay off their creditors. This is called

Chapter Eleven in the United States. If the company can find no other solution it goes into Chapter Seven and is liquidated. (See **Chapter Seven/Chapter Eleven**).

Barter. The act of exchanging one good for another, such as vodka for Pepsi. Barter allows traders to avoid the problems of unconvertible or hard-to-exchange currencies. In most developed countries, barter is unnecessary because it is much easier to use money as a go-between.

Basis Point. A hundred of these make one percentage point. Financial markets have become so finely tuned that it is no longer enough to talk about interest rates going up one quarter or a sixteenth of a percent. They often move by as little as a hundredth of a percent, or one basis point. A half of a percent rise in a bond's yield, 0.5 percent, is fifty basis points.

Bear Market/Bull Market. A bear, growling and pessimistic, is used to describe a declining market. A bull, charging optimistically ahead, symbolizes a rising market.

Bearer Bond. The ultimate transferable security, bearer bonds are understandably the payment of choice for villains in James Bond movies: there is no owner's name or registration for a bearer bond, so they can be cashed with no questions asked. The holder has the right to the full value of the bond, plus interest payments. Most international securities, such as Eurobonds, are issued in bearer form.

Big Bang. In Japan, the expression "big bang" was used to refer to a package of financial reforms undertaken in 1998. It had previously been used to describe the deregulation of London's securities market that led to an explosion in banking and financial services when many international banks and trading moved to "The City" to take advantage of the opportunities for trading large blocks of securities with no restrictions or taxes imposed by the local authorities.

Bilateral Trade Agreements. When two countries get together to regulate trade in goods and/or services. Bilateral trade agreements are gradually falling out of favor—countries usually prefer more inclusive "multilateral" accords.

Black Markets. Wherever a desired good is prohibited by law, black markets tend to spring up. In some currencies, where currency exchange is prohibited, for example, black markets take over the normal role of banks—often with little or no police interference. The black economy consists of all those underground transactions that, because of their illegality, go unreported.

Blue Chip. AAA, top of the line. A blue-chip stock is one that is considered the best in its field. The term originated in the game of poker—where the most expensive chips are usually the blue ones.

Bond. The ultimate IOU. A bond is a piece of paper that says, "I, the borrower, promise to pay you, the bond owner, a certain amount of money in the future." The little pieces of paper we call bonds, along with their electronic counterparts, can be bought and sold among investors all over the world. Whoever owns the bond also has the right to periodic interest payments.

Bourse. The word *bourse,* which means "purse" in French, has come to mean "stock market" in most countries around the world.

Brady Bond. Named after the former U.S. Treasury Secretary, Brady bonds are repackaged debt issued by Third World countries that have fallen on hard times. Brady Bonds have the backing of U.S. Treasury Securities, which makes them more attractive to international investors.

Bridge Loan. A bridge over troubled waters. As the name implies, bridge loans cover a short span of time, allowing the borrower time to arrange more long-lasting financing. The International Monetary Fund and the Bank for International Settlements often provide bridge loans to poor countries trying to arrange bailouts with the World Bank or other long-term lenders.

Broker/Dealer. Just as a real estate broker brings together buyers and sellers for a fee, a securities broker acts as a go-between in financial transactions. Most brokers—stock brokers, for example—receive a commission based on the volume of securities traded. A dealer, on the other hand, has an inventory of goods that can be sold to investors. Some investment bankers fill both roles and are called, not surprisingly, broker/dealers.

Bundesbank. Germany's central bank, before the establishment of the European Central Bank, was the prime guardian of the German economy. The word means "Federal Bank" in German. The Bundesbank still takes care of domestic German monetary policy and financial market regulation.

C2C. Consumer to consumer transactions on the Web allow individuals to avoid buying goods and services from businesses. By going to an online auction site, for example, consumers buy and sell directly from each other—for a small fee to the auction site, of course. Some analysts say that letting consumers bid for goods and services, such as last-minute concert tickets or airline seats, is a form of consumer-to-business transaction—which would be called C2B. (See **B2B, B2C**).

Call Option. A call option gives the holder the right to buy something at a certain price. Like other options, a call option can only be exercised for a certain length of time. An investor who thinks the price of an asset will go up will buy call options. As the underlying security goes up in price, so does the call option. Investors can buy call and put options (see **Put Option**) on such diverse instruments as stocks, commodities, and foreign currencies.

Capital Gain. When securities or real estate are sold at a profit, the difference between the sale price and the original purchase price is called a capital gain. Capital gains are usually taxed at different rates from other income such as interest and dividend payments. In some countries, capital gains are not taxed at all.

Capital Market. Where investors go to buy or sell securities. A capital market is an exchange or a group of exchanges where bonds and other long-term debt instruments are traded. Most capital market trading is not done on official exchanges, but on trading floors in banks scattered around the world and connected electronically to form one big international market.

Capitalism. The economic system that allows private ownership and lets the markets make the decisions on how much to produce and at what price.

Cartel. A group of companies or countries that band together to control production and prices. The most famous example of a cartel in the world economy is OPEC (see **OPEC**) that was set up in 1960 to coordinate the production of oil, thus allowing better control over the market price.

Cash Cow. A company or a stock that generates a continuous flow of cash is called a cash cow. Usually, cash cows don't need any marketing or special attention, they just keep churning out the profits.

Cash Crops/Food Crops. In many developing countries, a food crop is often used only for feeding the farmer's family. If there is a surplus, it can be sold for cash—hence, the name cash crop—which provides money for the family to buy clothing, shelter, and other items necessary for survival.

Cash Flow. A quick measure of the money coming into and going out of a company. Cash flow tells investors what the company has done over a specific period of time, without accounting tricks, such as depreciation and other write-offs.

Centrally Planned Economies. Where the bureaucrats make the decisions. In a centrally planned economy, the state has the authority to decide who produces what and at what price it will be sold. Prices and resource allocation are also decided by the central decision-making bodies. The goal is to make the economy more equitable, but the result is often increased waste and inefficiency. Centrally planned economies are also called command economies or planned economies.

Chaebol. In South Korea, many companies are grouped together in conglomerates, or "chaebols," that sometimes become quasi-monopolies. After the economic crisis of the late 1990s, the Korean government moved to dismantle them.

Chapter Seven, Chapter Eleven. The two most important concepts in the book of bankruptcy (see **Bankruptcy**). In the U.S., Chapter Eleven, called Administration in Britain, allows a bankrupt company to try to work out its troubles. Chapter Seven, called Receivership in Britain, is when the struggling company is liquidated—the assets are sold off to pay as many of the company's debts as possible.

The City, Wall Street, Bahnhofstrasse, Kabuto-cho. The part of London where most of the banks and securities houses are located is usually simply referred to as the City of London. The British financial community is often simply referred to as The City. In New York, they use the term "Wall Street" to describe the financial community as a whole. In Zurich, it's the "Bahnhofstrasse." In Tokyo, it's the "Kabuto-cho." When Venice was the center of the world economy—back in the Middle Ages—the banks were all clustered around the Rialto Bridge. Hence, Shylock's famous line in Shakespeare's *The Merchant of Venice*: "What news on the Rialto?"

Command Economies. An economy where the government calls all the shots, from how much is produced to how much consumers are allowed to purchase (see **Centrally Planned Economies**).

Commercial Bank. A bank that takes deposits and makes loans; what one traditionally thinks of when one thinks of a bank. Although commercial banks—in Japan and the United States, mainly—have been prohibited in the past from getting involved in investment banking activities such as selling stocks or underwriting IPOs, they can now do almost anything investment banks can.

Commodity. Raw materials, such as oil, gas, or orange juice, are called commodities. Commodities are easily traded on the world markets because they are relatively homogenous: gold from Siberia is basically the same as gold from Nevada. Commodities can be traded in many ways: in spot transactions, for immediate delivery, or in the futures market, where they are traded at a price that will be effective at some later date. Other commodities: silver, tin, beef, wheat—and the proverbial pork belly.

Common Market. The European Union was once called the Common Market. The idea, at the time, was to simply allow goods and money to flow, unrestricted, across members' borders. When the "European Community" became a political entity as well as economic, it was decided to change its name to "European Union."

Communism. "From each according to his abilities, to each according to his needs." Communism's goal was—and still is, in some countries—to create a society with total equality. This utopian idea, developed during the nineteenth century by economic philosophers such as Karl Marx, attempts to find an alternative to the abuses of the capitalist system— especially egregious during the early years of the Industrial Revolution.

Comparative Advantage. Doing what you do best. Comparative advantage is an economic theory that is based on the idea that if a country excels in one particular activity—making movies, for example, or growing grapes—it should be allowed to do it for everyone. It is assumed that each country will find some thing it is better at than the others. In this way, the country that makes the best wine can send wine abroad and get bread, cheese, or CD-ROM in return.

Consumer Price Index (CPI). Governments keep track of the prices of goods and services in order to determine inflation in an economy. By looking at the price of haircuts, gasoline, bread, and a whole "basket" of other products, governments can determine how much prices are going up in the economy as a whole. This index, called the CPI in the United States and the Retail Price Index in Britain, is then used to readjust fixed incomes such as pensions and social security payments.

Convention on International Trade in Endangered Species (CITES). Along with the United Nations Environment Program (UNEP), the CITES group regulates the trade in endangered species of wild fauna and flora. By controlling the sale of ivory, for example, poaching can be reduced to a minimum. CITES makes a distinction between animals that need to be protected by a total ban on trade and hunting, called Appendix I, and those species of animals that can be "harvested" in sustainable numbers, called Appendix II.

Convergence. Individual countries often have divergent economic needs, so governments try to homogenize the economy as much as possible. Just as it's hard for the Fed to balance the needs of each region of the United States—California could be booming, for example, while the Northeast stagnates—it is extremely difficult for the European Central Bank to treat all the various countries of the European Union as a single economic zone. The member countries decided, therefore, to try to make the different economies converge as much as possible, especially in the areas of inflation, growth, and unemployment.

Convertible Bond. To make bonds or other securities more attractive to investors, companies sometimes make them convertible, allowing investors to exchange them for something else of value, usually company shares. A convertible bond is a sort of option: the owner has the right, but not the obligation, to trade the bond in any time during the life of the bond.

Corporate Finance. When companies or governments need to borrow money, they usually turn to investment banks to help them find financing at the best price. The expense of this advice is usually compensated by reduced costs of borrowing in the international markets. The goal of a corporate finance advisor is to find the right mix of bonds, equity, swaps, and other loans and securities that allow the borrower to secure funding at the lowest possible cost.

Correction. A temporary market drop. Contrary to a crash, which is expected to last, a market correction is the way economists describe a short-term decline in the value of stocks or bonds.

Creative Destruction. New technologies push out old ones. This economic theory formulated by Joseph Schumpeter way back in the 1930s foresaw the New Economy revolution. Schumpeter theorized that economies grew by leaps, and if businesses didn't adapt to new technologies, new kinds of products, and new ways of producing and distributing goods, then they would be destroyed, which means to say they would go out of business.

Cum. In Latin, *cum* means "with." A bond with a warrant still attached to it is referred to as "cum." A stock sold with the dividend still to be paid is traded, "cum dividend."

Currency. A mark, a yen, a buck, or a pound—printed money is the currency of advanced industrial economies. Most currencies are nothing more than a promise by a country's central bank written on pretty paper. In the United States, the Treasury's promise used to include the option to exchange the dollar for gold. Since 1973, this is no longer the case. Now most major currencies are only worth what other people or businesses are willing to pay or trade for them.

Current Account/Capital Account. A country's current account measures its international trade in goods and services over a given period. Current accounts measure "visible" trade, such as apples and television sets, as well as "invisible" trade, such as banking services and movies. The current account also includes financial transfers, such as money sent home by someone working abroad, payments to international organizations, and interest payments on a country's foreign debt. The current account is balanced by the "capital account," which includes all transfers of money in the opposite direction.

Datsu-sara. The Japanese had to invent a word to describe Japanese managers who leave a company to go somewhere else. It used to be a rare occurrence, but with today's global economy no one can expect to be a *sarariman,* working for the same company forever. *Datsu-sara* literally means "corporate dropout."

Dealer. See **Broker/Dealer.**

Debenture. A debenture is any bond backed only by the good credit of the company issuing it. It is an IOU that can be negotiated like any other security. The purchaser of a debenture relies on the full faith and credit of the issuer to be paid back, which means that they are only paid off after other, more senior debt has been taken care of. "Subordinated debentures" naturally provide a higher rate of interest to reward investors for the higher risk.

Debt Ratio or Debt/Equity Ratio. A good way to judge a company's health is to look at how much it owes and how much it owns. The basic idea of a debt ratio is that if a company owes too much money to creditors it will have a hard time staying afloat unless it has investors who are patient about getting paid back. In the New Economy companies, debt ratios are extremely high. A new company often needs many years to start earning money before it can begin paying back loans.

Default. When a company or a country is not able to pay its creditors on time, it is said to be in default. The interest payments on notes and bonds are usually the first to be stopped by a cash-strapped borrower. If no solution is found, the company is forced to file bankruptcy. A country in default sees its credit rating plummet and will find it difficult to get any more funds from international investors.

Deficit. Almost too good to be true, deficit spending allows you to pay more out than you receive. In the world economy, there are two kinds of deficits: budget deficits and trade deficits. A government runs a budget deficit when tax revenues are not enough to pay for spending. To cover budget deficit spending, a government either issues debt—such as treasury bonds—or simply prints up more money. When a country spends more on imports than it earns from exports, it runs a trade deficit.

Deflation. The opposite of inflation. Deflation is the percentage decline in the costs of a chosen basket of goods and services in a country. Deflation rarely occurs because most companies are usually reluctant to cut prices. Not to be confused with disinflation, which is a slowing down of the rate of inflation.

Demand. Demand is the part of economics relating to consumption. Essentially, demand tells us what consumers or businesses will buy at a given price. Economists use complicated supply and demand curves to explain this very basic concept: when producers raise their prices, demand falls. Conversely, when prices are reduced, demand increases. It's that simple.

Depreciation. Accountants call the reduction of an asset's value over time depreciation. As a car or a computer loses its value over the years, this has to be reflected in the company's books. Tax authorities allow companies to treat depreciation as cost of doing business, thus reducing their taxable income. Companies prefer to depreciate as much as they can as early as they can in order to reduce their tax bill.

Depression. A prolonged economic slowdown. A depression is marked by a steep decline in production and demand. As a result, stock markets drop, more companies go bankrupt, and unemployment rises. Governments try to avoid depressions by providing the necessary stimuli, such as increasing the money supply or increasing government spending. The Great Depression of the 1930s, caused in part by trade wars, made it clear—even then—how interconnected the world economy is.

Deregulation. *Que sera, sera.* "Whatever will be, will be." When governments want to encourage competition and make economies more productive, they often deregulate, removing restrictions on companies' behavior. After deregulation, companies such as airlines or telephone service providers are allowed to make their own decisions on prices and markets, regardless of the effect on consumers.

Derivative. A financial instrument that gets its value from other financial instruments. A derivative, such as an option or an index-tracking future, will increase in value whenever the value of the underlying security or securities on which it is based goes up. It may sound like a house of cards, but derivatives are nothing more than securities that allow people to invest in different ways. Derivatives are risky because they give investors more bang for the buck, allowing them to benefit big if the underlying instrument goes up in value, and lose big if it goes down.

Devaluation. Some governments use open-market purchases and interest rate policy to support their currencies on the international markets. When speculators and other international investors start selling a currency they perceive to be weak, a government has two choices: use more resources to keep the currency at the desired level, or let the currency's value fall to a new level—which is called devaluation. Devaluations occur everywhere, from Brazil to Thailand, from Indonesia to England.

Diminishing Returns. Imagine walking out of the desert and being asked how much you would be willing to pay for your first bottle of Coca-Cola. Most producers and consumers are willing to pay a lot for the first item—a new car, for example—

but the law of diminishing returns shows that producers have to keep reducing the price of any good or service in order to get the consumer to buy "just one more." In a factory, new machinery is also subject to the laws of diminishing returns: when the first machines are installed, productivity usually increases rapidly. When additional machines are installed, productivity still increases, but not as quickly.

Discount Rate. The interest rate that central banks charge for loans to banks and other financial institutions. The discount rate is regarded as a benchmark, in that other interest rates in an economy are based on it. It is closely watched because its movement gives a fairly accurate indication of the direction of interest rates throughout the economy. In the United States, the Federal Reserve sets the discount rate. This is not to be confused with the Fed Funds Rate, which is what banks charge each other for overnight loans.

Disinflation. A slowdown in the rate of inflation. This term is often confused with "deflation" (see **Deflation**), which is an actual decline in prices. Disinflation simply means that prices aren't rising as quickly as they were.

Disinvestment. Another way of saying "privatization." A government disinvests when it sells off state-owned industries. The idea is that the companies will be better managed once they are in private hands. The money earned from disinvestment also helps many a cash-strapped government.

Dividend. A payment to a company's shareholders. A dividend usually occurs when a company has made a profit and instead of reinvesting the money into the company—which would tend to make the share price rise—it is paid out to shareholders. Dividends can also be in the form of stock or other securities.

Division of Labor. A butcher, a baker, a candlestick maker—when an economy divides up work, letting each worker "do what they do best," things usually get done more efficiently. All modern economies are based on the principle of division of labor.

Dormant Account. An inactive bank account. In Switzerland, many of the accounts that were not claimed after World War II were simply left inactive, earning little or no interest. Meanwhile, family members struggled—often in vain—to find all the documents required by the Swiss banks in order to get access to these dormant accounts. Only after international pressure in the late 1990s forced the Swiss banks to reveal that thousands of these "sleeping" accounts still existed did the truth come out. The Swiss banks then made a multibillion dollar settlement with Holocaust survivors and their representatives to make up for their previous lack of cooperation.

Dow Jones Industrial Average (DJIA). The Dow Jones index is the most watched market index in the world. Even though it tracks the prices of only 30 blue-chip stocks, it is seen as a true indicator of the stock market as a whole. It used to include only "old economy" stocks from the New York Stock Exchange. Then it began to add NASDAQ's "New Economy" stocks, such as Intel and Microsoft. Dow Jones also produces indexes for other types of stocks, such as transportation and utilities.

Dumping. The sale of goods or services at a price below cost. The United States has accused many countries of trying to buy market share by selling goods in America at prices that are below those charged in the producer's home country. Some countries call U.S. anti-dumping laws a "cover" for protectionism. The American government, despite its claims to be a leader in trade liberalization, has often used "dumping" as an excuse for high tariffs on a wide variety of goods, from Brazilian shoes to South Korean steel.

Earnings. A company's earnings are its proverbial bottom line. Earnings are what is left after subtracting all the expenses from revenue. Earnings are sometimes also called net income, or, more simply, profits.

Econometrics. The scientific use of statistics and formulas to develop economic theories. Econometricians use complex mathematical models to simulate real-life situations and test the effects of a wide-range of variables such as interest rates, taxes, and investment.

Economy of Scale. "Many hands make light work." Economy of scale is an advantage that comes from making a lot of the same thing at once. Who would ever bake just one cookie, or teach a class with just one student? Henry Ford's first automobile assembly plant used this idea of mass production to produce large quantities of Model T's—and offered them in great numbers at low prices. Producing in large numbers means that the initial cost of investment is spread out over a large number of products or services.

ECU. The European Currency Unit was invented by the countries of the European Union in an effort to facilitate accounting between the member states. It was based on a basket of currencies from each of the EU member countries. The ECU was later eclipsed by the euro.

Elasticity. The measure of how much something will change or stretch in a given situation. Elasticity of demand, for example, tells how much the demand for a given product will change if there is a change in price. A shopper with a high elasticity of demand will rush out and buy a product as soon as it goes on sale.

Emerging Economies. See Third World.

Environmental Defense. An environmental group based in the United States that is active in trying to limit pollution by using economic incentives, such as road-pricing, to discourage automobile use. Web site: www.edf.org.

Equilibrium. Classical economics is based on the theory that all forces in an economy move toward an equilibrium. When the price of a product is too high, for example, people will stop buying it. In order to make more sales, the producer has to lower the price, and keep lowering it until demand and supply are in equilibrium. Equilibriums exist for many economic concepts, such as savings, investment, and employment.

Equity. Equity means ownership: a stockholder has equity in a company just as a homeowner has equity in a house. On a company's balance sheet, equity refers to the part of a company that belongs to the shareholders after all liabilities have been subtracted from assets. A company's net worth is called "stockholders' equity."

Euro. The new currency on the block. The euro was created by the European Union on January 1, 1999 when eleven countries in the European Union fixed their currencies to a totally new unit of exchange. From that point on, the national currencies of Germany, France, Italy, Spain, Portugal, Ireland, Austria, Finland, Belgium, Luxembourg, and the Netherlands existed no more than on paper—the actual notes and bills would only be put into circulation in 2002. Britain, Denmark, and Sweden held out, preferring to "wait and see." Greece was allowed to join in 2000.

Eurodollar. A "currency abroad," Eurodollars are U.S. dollars held in bank accounts outside the United States. The prefix "euro" can be applied to any currency held outside its country of origin, even if the country abroad isn't in Europe. Japanese yen held in Singapore, for example are Euroyen, just as British pounds held in Canada are called Europounds. What do you call a euro that is held outside of Europe? A Euro-euro.

Euromarkets. The restriction-free markets for securities trading, centered mainly in London, are called Euromarkets. The Eurobond market, for example, allows issuers and investors to buy and sell a wide variety of securities, free from the restrictions of local authorities.

European Central Bank (ECB). Based in Frankfurt, the ECB was set up in the late 1990s to oversee economic and monetary policy in the eleven countries that had adopted the euro. It was clear that without a common interest rate and money supply policy, the individual member states would all tend to go their own way and the new currency would have no chance of succeeding.

European Union. The European Union—previously called the European Community or Common Market—began as a simple customs union. The original idea was to do away with barriers to trade between the member countries. Eventually, this evolved into a broader union, with common political, social, and economic policies.

Ex. The Latin term meaning "from" is used to describe bonds or stocks that have had their warrants removed or dividends already paid. A stock that is sold "ex" is one that has already had its dividend distributed to a previous owner. (See **Cum.**)

Exchange Rates. The value of currencies worldwide is provided by exchange rates, which tell you what each currency is worth in terms of other currencies. Just like any other commodity, a currency is worth whatever people will pay for it. In the foreign exchange market, this involves putting two currencies together. A Norwegian krone, for example, is worth a fixed amount of euros or dollars or yen. Exchange rates are constantly being readjusted to keep them in line with the everchanging markets.

Fair Labor Association (FLA). One of many human-rights groups active on college campuses, the FLA has worked to build a coalition of companies, consumers, and social activists to find a solution to the sweatshop conditions in factories in developing countries. The idea is to develop a comprehensive strategy for upgrading the whole apparel industry so that workers are protected by a set of rules governing such areas as freedom of association, minimum wages, maximum working hours, bathrooms, and safety. Web site:www.fairlabor.org.

Fed Funds. The interest rate that banks in the United States charge on overnight loans to other banks is called the "fed funds rate" because the money being loaned is usually kept at the Federal

Reserve. When a bank has excess reserves at the Fed, it can loan this money to other banks that need to meet the Fed's stringent reserve requirements. The Fed Funds rate is often confused with the Discount rate, which is set by the Federal Reserve. The Fed Funds rate is, in fact, set by the banks themselves.

Federal Open Market Committee. Economic and monetary policy in the United States is controlled, in large part, by a small group of Federal Reserve Board members that meet on a regular basis. Essentially, the Fed Open Market Committee is in charge of deciding how quickly the economy will be allowed to grow.

Federal Reserve. The United States' central bank, the Federal Reserve, manages the money supply, regulates the banking system, and acts as a lender of last resort to banks in trouble. The Federal Reserve is independent; it answers to no one, except in its yearly report to Congress. The seven members of the Federal Reserve Board are appointed by the president.

Financial Action Task Force (FATF). Based in Paris, the Financial Action Task Force is an independent organization that examines tax havens around the world and issues regular reports on which countries are not cooperating in the fight against money laundering. Web site: www.oecd.org/fatf.

The Financial Stability Forum. Based in Basel, Switzerland, the Financial Stability Forum was set up by the G7—the seven "rich" country governments—to promote financial stability and other matters of concern to the international markets, which includes keeping an eye on money laundering. Web site: www.fsforum.org.

Fiscal Policy. In contrast to monetary policy, which is in the hands of central bankers and other monetary authorities, a country's fiscal policy is in the hands of the elected government, which gets to decide how much to tax, how much to spend, and how much to borrow.

Flight Capital. Fearing economic turmoil or government policies that threaten savings, concerned citizens often send money to financial havens outside the country. This "flight capital" sometimes amounts to a large percentage of a country's total wealth. Latin Americans, for example, during times of high inflation, often buy dollars and send them to bank accounts abroad, usually in defiance of exchange control laws. Attempts by government to control transfers of money abroad often end up encouraging the practice of capital flight—exactly what they are trying to avoid.

Floating Rate Note (FRN). Like a home loan with an adjustable interest rate, a floating rate note is a debt security that has its interest rate changed from time to time. Most floating rate notes use LIBOR, the London InterBank Offered Rate, as a reference for determining the interest rate to be paid to the holder. Many banks and investors prefer the price stability of floating rate notes. During periods of fluctuating interest rates, the prices of FRNs remain relatively stable because in order to remain in line with prevailing interest rates, floating rate notes change their interest payments, not their price.

Foreign Direct Investment (FDI). The total of all foreign investment in a country's economy. It includes "green-field" investments such as new factories and power plants, and "paper" investments, such as buying shares of existing companies.

Foreign Exchange (F/X). In the foreign exchange markets, currencies are traded against each other. A dollar is quoted in terms of how many euros or yen each dollar is worth. "Forex" market trading takes place twenty-four hours a day, usually on specialized bank trading floors that are electronically connected with other exchanges throughout the world.

Forest Stewardship Council (FSC). The watchdog of the world's tropical forests. The Forest Stewardship Council was set up to provide consumers in the world economy—businesses as well as individuals—with an official seal of approval. Wood or wood products with the FSC seal were harvested in accordance with the standards set up by the World Wildlife Fund. The FSC ensures that wood is being cut in ways that ensure sustainability: instead of clear-cutting, for example, only selected trees are cut, keeping the forest intact. Web site: www.fscus.org.

Forward Markets. A forward contract fixes the price of a future transaction. A wheat farmer, for example, can sell next year's harvest by going to the forward markets to find someone who will make a price today. Unlike futures contracts, which are traded on exchanges with fixed prices and dates, forward contracts can be tailor-made to accommodate the needs of the buyers and the sellers.

Free Market. A free-market economy, where the decisions are left up to the market, not the government, ends up—in theory—providing consumers and businesses with the best products at the best prices. In contrast to centrally planned economies where decisions on how much to produce and how to distribute that production are made by the government, a free-market economy lets the markets decide everything from prices to production.

Free Trade Area of the Americas (FTAA). In a meeting in Miami in 1994, Western Hemisphere leaders decided to join together all of the disparate trading groups, from the Yukon to Tierra del Fuego, and create a "Free Trade Area of the Americas," which would eventually encompass all of the free-market economies of North, Central, and South America.

Friedman, Milton. The doyen of free-market economists. Milton Friedman, Nobel Prize winner and University of Chicago economist, has done more than anyone in the world to promote the idea that free markets are the best way to make economic decisions. For decades, he has called for worldwide expansion of free trade and capitalism from Chile to the Ukraine. "The freedom to choose" is the goal of "Friedmanian" economics: if consumers are allowed to buy what they want and producers are free to sell where they want, the world will be made a better place for all.

Future. A future is a contract to buy or sell a commodity or financial instrument at a fixed price at a fixed time in the future. Futures are unlike forward contracts in that they have fixed prices and fixed dates. Because the time and date conform to other contracts, futures can be traded on exchanges (see **Stock Index Future**).

G7/G8/G20/G77. The Group of Seven, G7, began by bringing together leaders once a year to informal meetings where they could discuss economic issues. It is called the G8 whenever Russia participates. The seven main members—the United States, Canada, Japan, Germany, Italy, Britain, and France—also decided to create a larger group, called the G20, which includes representatives from the developing countries as well. Another organization, the Group of 77, brings together only leaders of the developing countries.

Game Theory. A way of looking at the world as if it were a game, with clear winners and losers (see **Zero-Sum Game**).

GATT. The precursor to the World Trade Organization. The General Agreement on Tariffs and Trade laid the groundwork for the WTO to oversee the global trade in goods and services.

GDP/GNP. Gross domestic product (GDP) and gross national product (GNP) are both measures of economic activity. Whereas GDP measures all of a country's domestic production of goods and services, GNP adds in the international components, including income from foreign operations. Neither GDP nor GNP tells the whole story, however. Many economies have unreported activities—including unpaid housework, volunteer work, and a lot of illegal activities such as drug sales and prostitution. GDP and GNP are often used interchangeably. Another word for GDP/GNP is *output*.

Gearing. Getting more bang for your buck. Gearing refers to the amount of debt a company has in relation to its share capital. This is also called debt ratio. Just as a bicycle uses a bigger gear on the front sprocket to make the rear wheel go faster, a company can increase its debt to make the stockholders' funds go further. Many dot-com startups have learned the hard way that gearing is not always the best solution. A highly geared company may get into trouble if it isn't generating enough cash to pay the interest payments on the increased debt.

Gold Standard. It used to be that a currency's value was either fixed by the government or linked to some other item of value. For example, until 1973 in the United States dollars could be converted into gold. This gold standard was meant to guarantee that currencies would always have a certain value, determined by the amount of gold held in each country's vaults. This is no longer the case.

Golden Parachute. Fearing a hostile takeover, many managers incorporate huge guaranteed salary hikes and bonuses into their severance packages—to ensure that they'll land on their feet (with their pockets full of money) should they ever be forced out of their job.

Greenmail. In a takeover or leveraged buyout, companies sometimes get opponents to change their course of action through "greenmail," offering them financial incentives such as buying back their shares at above-market prices.

Hedge. A hedge provides a barrier or protection from an uncertain event in the future. Homeowners, for example, feel safe knowing that in times of high inflation, their real estate will go up in value, hedging other losses. An owner of a stock portfolio can hedge by buying put options, which give the right to sell at a higher price if the market should drop.

Hedge Fund. Only remotely related to the practice of hedging, hedge funds borrow money to make big, speculative investments, usually in areas that banks and traditional investors shy away from. Famous hedge fund investors like George Soros and Long-Term Capital Management have had spectacular success—and spectacular failures—investing in such arcane areas as Russian currency markets, oil prices and yield differentials between different kinds of U.S. Treasury bonds. Hedge funds earn billions—and lose billions—overnight, often by using computer models that purportedly are smarter than the market.

High Net Worth Individual. The kind of client most banks dream about. A high net worth individual is one who has a lot of disposable assets and few liabilities. Banks around the world have discovered that having this type of client can be a lucrative business. In New York, London, Paris, Geneva, Luxembourg, Tokyo, Singapore, Hong Kong, and Zurich, banks have set up special facilities for high net worth clients.

Hot Money. Money invested for short periods is referred to as "hot" money. In developing countries, billions of dollars can come flooding in, in search of high returns. When the economic fundamentals change, however, the money can flow out again at a moment's notice.

Human Development Index (HDI). Economic statistics only tell part of the story. The Human Development Index was developed by the United Nations Development Program to track countries' efforts to escape from poverty. It examines such factors as average age, literacy, and standard of living. The UN Human Development Index tries to look beyond the standard data of economic growth and financial profit to show us how economies are actually contributing to the well-being of their people.

Hyperinflation. Prices rising out of control. Hyperinflation usually occurs in countries with severe economic problems, such as Germany in the 1920s and many countries in Latin America in the 1990s. In some hyperinflationary countries, prices can rise more than one thousand percent per year.

Import Substitution. Governments sometimes use protective tariffs or quotas to force businesses and consumers to substitute imports with locally produced goods and services. This policy of import substitution is often implemented in developing countries in an effort to save precious foreign currency reserves and promote economic development. The problem is that many countries can't produce all goods at the same level of quality as imported goods. When a government forces farmers to buy poorly made local tractors, for example, it can reduce crop yields, and everyone suffers.

Incomes Policy. Incomes policy is an inflation-control plan that countries use to reduce consumers' real disposable income. Freezing wages is one example: by reducing spending, it is hoped, the economy slows down and prices are brought under control.

Inflation. Inflation is the percentage increase in prices. In most economies, inflation is measured by an index of consumer prices, such as the Consumer Price Index (CPI) in the United States and the Retail Price Index (RPI) in Britain.

Initial Public Offering. See IPO.

Insider Trading. A company's insiders are those who have advance knowledge of financial statements or other company secrets. In some countries, insider trading is tolerated with the rationale that someone has to be the first to trade on new information, so why not let the insiders be the ones? This "first come, first serve" mentality is losing sway, however; insider trading is now illegal in every major world economy.

Institutional Investors. Contrary to small "retail" investors, institutional investors such as insurance companies and pension funds invest billions of dollars—or yens or euros or pesos—in the world economy every day. Their decisions dwarf most other players in the international markets, including many governments.

Interbank Market. The interbank rate that banks charge for loans to other banks is usually the lowest in the market. These interbank interest rates are then used as a benchmark, or standard, for other lending.

International Development Association (IDA). The arm of the

World Bank that lends to the world's poorest countries under generous conditions. Contributions from wealthy nations and privileged access to international capital markets provide the IDA with most of its funding.

International Labor Organization (ILO). Based in Geneva, the ILO is responsible for overseeing the aspects of the world economy that relate to labor. One of the major goals of the ILO is to make sure that workers in developing countries are provided with minimum standards and rights.

International Monetary Fund (IMF). The International Monetary Fund was established in 1945, at the same time as the World Bank. Its first job was to regulate the world's exchange rates. It has now assumed a leading role in restructuring debtor countries' economies and providing short-term loans to economies in need.

Internet Corporation for Assigned Names and Numbers (ICANN). ICANN oversees the system of Web domain-names such as .com and .org. Some ICANN directors are chosen by Internet service providers and some are elected by "netizens," ordinary Web users from around the world.

Internet Engineering Task Force (IETF). IETF develops technical standards for the Web. It is also a clearinghouse for getting users to agree on common standards.

Investment. Economists use the word investment to describe the part of economic production that is not saved or consumed. Accountants use the word to refer to a company's purchase of productive assets such as factories, equipment, vehicles, and computers.

Investment Bank. "Masters of the Universe." Investment banks in the United States used to have the monopoly for underwriting new issues of securities such as stocks and bonds. They often made a fortune trading these securities for their clients, as well as for themselves. Since investment-banking activity is considered riskier than traditional commercial banking, consisting mainly of taking deposits and making loans, investment banks have often been carefully separated from commercial banks. The United States and Japan are now moving toward the system used in Europe where "universal banks" are allowed to undertake both commercial and investment banking activities.

Invisible Hand. The idea that there is an invisible hand guiding the markets was formulated by the economic philosopher Adam Smith in the eighteenth century. His theory was that markets, if left to themselves, would find the most efficient way of doing things. This invisible hand is, in fact, the result of millions of profit-seeking consumers and producers making rational decisions in the marketplace.

Invisible Trade. Exports and imports of services such as banking, insurance, and media are defined as "invisible" because they aren't actually shipped abroad. Invisible trade can be anything from banking services to tourism to online music. In many economies, invisible trade has become more profitable than the trade in merchandise like commodities and machines.

(IPO) Initial Public Offering. When a dot-com or another type of company "goes public," its shares are sold and traded on a recognized exchange. This has the advantage of opening up a huge new investor pool, not to mention putting a lot of money into the hands of the original owners—but it also involves more bureaucratic work, including publishing accounting statements quarterly.

Joint Venture. Two or more companies joining forces in order to get a competitive advantage in a particular market. A foreign company will often enter a joint venture with a local company to take advantage of the partner's local knowledge and skills.

Junk Bonds. Companies with low credit ratings—below BBB, for example—often have to issue bonds with high interest rates in order to get needed capital for expansion or takeovers. These lower-than-investment-grade bonds are often called "junk bonds," but the investment banks that issue them prefer to call them "high-yield securities."

Kereitsu. *Japan Inc.* Kereitsu describes the tightly organized system of interlocking companies in Japan. It involves multiple layers of businesses, banks, wholesalers, distributors, and brand-loyal retailers that allow them to limit the influence of foreigners on local markets.

Keynesian Economics. John Maynard Keynes, a British economist, was one of the most influential economic thinkers of the twentieth century. Keynes' ideas on using government spending to combat economic recession revolutionized modern economics. Keynesian economics calls for overspending, or "deficit spending," during an economic slowdown, and underspending, or creating budget surpluses, during times of too-rapid economic expansion. Most politicians are easily convinced to use deficit spending to stimulate the economy, but are decidedly un-Keynesian when it comes to spending less during periods of rapid economic growth.

Laffer Curve. Rumor has it that an economist, Arthur Laffer, drew a curve on a napkin to show that a reduction in taxes would lead to more taxes coming in, not less. His idea was that if a government reduced taxes, it would free up money that people would use more efficiently, thus stimulating the economy. This new economic activity was, in the end, supposed to bring in even more taxes. This theory, referred to as supply side economics, was tested during the Reagan administration and resulted in a doubling of the national debt.

Lagging Economic Indicators. Unemployment and GDP growth are called lagging economic indicators because they tell you where the economy has been, as opposed to Leading Economic Indicators, such as housing starts which tell you where the economy is headed. (See **Leading Economic Indicators.**)

Laissez Faire. The French term *laissez faire* means, literally, "let them do it." It is used to describe a government policy that lets the markets decide what is best. Consumers and producers, in theory, will come to the right decisions if they are left to decide on their own.

Leading Economic Indicators. Statistics that help an economy's leaders plot the course of future economic activity. Leading economic indicators track such things as retail sales, spending on new plants and machinery and housing starts. These indicators tell us where the economy is headed (see **Lagging Economic Indicators**).

Letter of Credit. In international trade, importers often need to prove that funds are available to pay for an incoming shipment of goods. This is usually provided by a bank in the form of a letter of credit, which guarantees the seller that funds are available to pay for the goods when they arrive.

Leveraged Buyout (LBO). A leveraged buyout uses borrowed money to take over a company. The buyer puts up a certain amount of money and borrows the rest. Just as a playground seesaw allows you to lift a large weight with a relatively small amount of strength, a leveraged buyout allows an investor to use a relatively small investment to buy a large company.

Liability. On a balance sheet, liabilities are lined up to the right of the assets. Liabilities typically include debt or other anticipated obligations—money that the company has to pay back sometime in the future. Current liabilities are those that have to be paid off in twelve months or less. Longer-term liabilities are referred to as long-term debt.

LIBOR. The London Interbank Offered Rate is one of the benchmarks for interest rates, like the Fed Funds Rate in the United States or the Lombard Rate. LIBOR is often used as a reference for determining interest rates throughout the world economy, from corporate loans to floating-rate notes.

Liquidity. In the trading world, liquidity means being able to execute trades with ease. Essentially, it means that there are enough buyers and sellers to guarantee a market. Liquidity can also mean there is a ready supply of funds. On a company's balance sheet, liquidity refers to the company's ability to come up with the cash to pay its debts.

Lombard Rate. The interest rate that central banks in some European countries charge on collateralized loans is called the Lombard Rate. The banks borrowing the money usually have to put up government bonds as collateral to receive the preferential Lombard rates. The name is based on Europe's early bankers, who, more often than not, came from Lombardia, the northern Italian region where Milan is located.

Macroeconomics. The "big picture." Macroeconomics is the study of an economy's aggregate factors, such as growth, unemployment, inflation, and government spending. The other side of the economy, the "small picture" of individuals and firms, is called microeconomics.

Margin. When investors are allowed to leverage their securities purchases, it is commonly referred to as "margin trading." In a margin account, banks or brokers loan money to investors so they can buy more stocks or bonds. The client puts up some of the money; the bank puts up the rest. For a relatively small investment, the rewards to the client can be enormous when markets go up. But when markets go down, the client can lose a lot as well. If the market drops too much, the bank gives the client a margin call, which essentially says that more money has to be deposited or the remaining securities will be sold immediately, before the market has a chance to go down any further.

Marginal Analysis. The study of behavior at the edges. In economics, marginal analysis looks at how people or firms behave when given the option of having or producing "one more" of something. The additional "one thin wafer" is not so appetizing if it immediately follows a big meal. Marginal consumption looks at what it would take, in terms of a lower price, to get a consumer to buy just one more.

Market Economy. The economic system where the market—workers, firms, and households acting without government coordination and guided essentially by self-interest—make the decision on how much any given good or service is produced—and at what price. (See **Free Market**.)

Market-Maker. "I bid 25 and offer 26. Whatta you wanna do? You wanna buy or you wanna sell?" A market-maker is a professional trader who makes a two-way price. The price that a market-maker is willing to pay for something, the bid price, is always slightly lower than the offer price. The market-maker makes money on the spread, buying low and selling high—all day long.

Marx, Karl. The father of Communism. The German economic philosopher and sociologist Karl Marx wrote *Das Kapital,* the first major work outlining the principals of the communist economic model. In it, he predicted the demise of capitalism and called for the creation of a socialist economic system, based on the following principal: "from each according to his abilities, to each according to his needs."

Mean, Median. The terms mean and median are often confused. The mean is the simple average, the one schoolchildren learn, which consists of simply adding up a list of numbers and dividing the total by the number of items in the list. This is used in most economic calculations, such as average per capita income. Sometimes, however, it is useful to look at the way figures are distributed. Like a highway median strip, in a series of numbers the median is the point at which 50 percent of the numbers are higher and 50 percent are lower.

Mercantilism. The economic policy of using consistent trade surpluses to accumulate wealth and power. A mercantilist economy emphasizes exports over imports. Mercantilist countries, such as Japan in the 1990s, concentrate on producing a lot of goods for export instead of focusing on domestic consumption. The idea is to end up with a lot of foreign reserves that can be used for savings and international investment.

Merchandise Trade Balance. The narrowest measure of a country's trade, the *merchandise trade balance,* counts only "visi-

ble" goods such as motorcycles, wine, and laptops—not services. This measure is often referred to in the press as the balance of trade, trade balance, or even trade surplus, even
though it is not as all encompassing as the current account
(see separate entry). Basically, the merchandise trade balance
only includes goods that can actually be loaded onto a ship,
an airplane, or some other means of transport.

Merchant Banking. The practice whereby a securities house
invests its own money in its clients. In some countries, an
investment bank is also referred to as a merchant bank.

Mergers and Acquisitions (M&A). Buying or selling companies,
or joining them together, is referred to in international banking circles as M&A. Many mergers and acquisitions are
fueled by the desire to benefit from increased synergy, benefit-
ing from each company's strengths.

Metcalfe's Law. The more the merrier. Metcalfe's law postulates
that the more people or organizations participate in a network, the more effective it becomes. This is particularly
appropriate in the New Economy where Web sites and online
exchanges work better when more participants get involved.
The law is based on the idea that the value of the network increases in a square: when the number of participants
increases by two, for example, the value of the network will
increase by four. In the digital economy, it is postulated, the
more businesses and citizens that get involved in any given
network, the more efficient it will become.

Microeconomics. The study of an economy's individuals and
firms is called microeconomics. It is the opposite of macroeconomics, which looks at the big picture. Microeconomics,
like a microscope, looks at the smaller things, such as the
behavior of individuals and how firms make their decisions
under various economic conditions.

Mobilization for Global Justice (MGJ). One of the groups that
criticizes the World Trade Organization for being a vehicle

for rampant globalization. At the WTO meeting in Seattle, in 2000, where a popular slogan was "trickle-down economics is like feeding horses oatmeal so that sparrows can feed on their dung," the MGJ called for an end to rampant globalization and third-world exploitation.

Monetarism. The economic theory based on the belief that changes in the money supply can control economic growth is called monetarism. Monetarists believe that inflation can best be controlled by reducing the money supply.

Monetary Policy. In contrast to fiscal policy, which is determined by government taxing and spending, monetary policy is decided by central banks, such as the U.S. Federal Reserve. By regulating the money supply and interest rates, monetary authorities can effectively control economic growth.

Money Market. Money markets provide a place to bring together short-term borrowers and lenders. Most short-term investments (such as treasury bills or fiduciary deposits) are traded on the world's money markets, which consist of trading floors in banks and securities houses scattered across the globe.

Money Supply. A country's money supply has several different components, ranging from coins and notes to deposits in savings and checking accounts. The money supply most talked about is called M1, which consists of all notes and coins in circulation, as well as money in easy-to-access bank accounts.

Monopoly. A monopoly consists of complete control of one sector of production within an economy. A sole producer of a good could, in theory, raise prices without limit. There are very few real monopolies—consumers generally find an alternative if prices get too high. For example, the OPEC oil producers thought they had a near-monopoly in the 1970s and dramatically raised prices. But many consumers were able to find alternate sources of energy. The anti-trust charges against Microsoft in the late 1990s referred to monopolistic behavior, but Bill Gates countered that Microsoft had, in fact, been lowering most prices, not raising them.

Moody's. One of the largest credit ratings services in the world, Moody's provides an up-to-date analysis of the financial health of countries, companies, and other borrowers in the world economy. Moody's stamp of top quality, "AAA," is only awarded to the world's most creditworthy borrowers. (Web site: www.moodysratings.com)

Most Favored Nation (MFN). A "preferred" status for most U.S. trade partners, now referred to as "PNTR" (see **Permanent Normal Trade Relations**).

Multilateral Trade Agreements. An agreement between three or more trading partners. Most multilateral trade agreements are made under the guidance of the World Trade Organization (WTO), the successor organization to the General Agreement on Tariffs and Trade (GATT).

Multinational. A company with operations outside its home country is called a multinational. Although scorned by some as symbols of "capitalist imperialism," multinationals usually bring needed capital and jobs into the countries where they set up business.

Mutual Fund. A mutual fund is a collection of bonds or stocks sold to investors as a single investment. The advantage of a mutual fund is that investors can diversify risk over a wide range of securities within a single investment vehicle. Mutual funds are especially appropriate for international investors in markets where information on companies and markets is not easily accessible.

NAFTA. The North American Free Trade Agreement opened up the borders of Canada, the United States, and Mexico to almost limitless trade in goods and services. Unlike other trade groups, such as the European Union, NAFTA allows no additional barriers to trade with countries outside the block. The long-term goal of NAFTA was to remove trade barriers from Alaska to Argentina (see **Free Trade Area of the Americas**).

NASDAQ. The world's first major electronic trading market, NASDAQ—National Association of Securities Dealers Automated Quotation System—grew to become one of the world's biggest stock exchanges by the end of the twentieth century, trading many of the New Economy stocks, such as Intel, Amazon.com, and Microsoft.

Net Asset Value (NAV). In order to calculate the true value of shares in a mutual fund or an open-end fund, it is necessary to add up all the fund's assets—such as securities and cash—and subtract all the liabilities. This is then divided by the total number of shares outstanding to give investors an idea of what each share in the fund is really worth.

Net Assets. What a company really owns. Net assets are what are left when all of a company's debts are subtracted from its assets. Stockholders regard net assets as the part of the company that belongs to them, also referred to as stockholders' equity or shareholders' equity.

Net Income. Subtracting all expenses from a company's revenue gives us an idea of what a company has earned over a given period of time. Net income is basically just another way of saying profit.

Net Worth. An individual's net worth is calculated by adding up the monetary value of all assets, such as houses and bank accounts, and subtracting liabilities, such as mortgages and credit card bills. The net worth of a company is calculated in the same way—by subtracting liabilities from assets. (See **Net Assets**).

Newly Industrialized Countries (NICs). The select group of developing countries that are on their way to joining the ranks of developed nations, NICs are considered to be the elite economies of the Third World. Most lists of Newly Industrialized Countries include: Argentina, Brazil, Chile, Mexico, Singapore, South Africa, South Korea, Taiwan, and Thailand.

OECD. The Organization of Economic Cooperation and Development, based in Paris, brings together all of the world's advanced industrial economies, including the United States, Canada, Mexico, Japan, South Korea, Australia, New Zealand, and most Western European countries. Besides providing statistics and documents of all aspects of the global economy, the OECD serves as a forum for discussions and coordination of economic policy.

Offshore Banking. Any banking activity that is free of domestic restrictions and regulations is referred to as offshore banking. To compete with offshore banking centers such as the Bahamas and the Cayman Islands, traditional banking centers such as London and New York have set up facilities to cater to the needs of clients interested in putting their money into tax-free accounts. Other offshore banking centers can be found in Luxembourg, Singapore, and Hong Kong.

Oligopsony. Unlike a monopoly, where one company or individual controls a specific market, an oligopsony is a group of companies or individuals that combine their forces to "corner the market."

OPEC. The Organization of Petroleum Exporting Countries was established in 1960 to coordinate the policies of most of the world's major oil producers such as Saudi Arabia, Iran, Kuwait, Venezuela, Nigeria, Libya, and Indonesia. (See **Cartel**).

Open Market Operation. Central banks use open market operations to buy and sell securities. This has the effect of controlling the money supply because money held at central banks, such as the U.S. Federal Reserve, is not considered to be part of the money supply. When central bank money is used to buy securities on the open market, the money supply is therefore increased. Alternatively, when central banks sell securities on the open market, the money supply is reduced by the amount paid into the central banks' vaults. Most of the securities bought and sold in open market operations are government bonds.

Output. Another word for Gross Domestic Product (See **GDP/GNP**).

Over-the-Counter (OTC). Over-the-counter shares usually trade electronically, not on established stock exchanges. Most over-the-counter stocks are for small companies that don't meet the strict financial requirements required for listing on the major exchanges. Electronic OTC exchanges include the USM (Unlisted Securities Market) in Britain and the Tokyo "Second Section" market in Japan.

Par. When a bond sells at 100 percent of its face or nominal value, it's said to trade "at par." For most bonds, par is $1,000. For fixed-income stocks, par is usually $100. The price of most bonds, however, does not stay at par. When interest rates rise or fall, the price of an older bond has to rise above par or fall below it to make the bond's return competitive with new bonds entering the market.

Paradigm. The rules of the game. By changing the rules governing how an economy works—introducing the Internet into all stages of production and distribution, for example—you shift the paradigm, which makes it "a whole new ball game."

Patent. The exclusive right to market a specific product or service. Without patent protection, companies would never invest the money—often totaling hundreds of millions of dollars—to develop new products and technologies like drugs and genetic engineering.

Per Capita. Latin for "per head." Per capita can also be translated as "per person." It is a vary useful concept for comparing countries because it puts all the figures on a human scale. Brazil may have a larger total debt than Argentina, but when this debt is distributed over the whole population, Brazil's per capita debt may end up being much smaller than its less-populated neighbor.

Perestroika. Russian for "economic restructuring," perestroika was the buzzword for Mikhail Gorbachev's daring plan for economic reform in the last years of the Soviet Union. Coupled with "glasnost," which called for more political openness, perestroika's goal was to make the economy more efficient by decentralizing decision-making.

Permanent Normal Trade Relations (PNTR). The new term for most favored nation trade status. When the United States gave PNTR status to China, the two parties agreed to remove all major barriers to trade.

Philips Curve. The economic principle that inflation is linked to unemployment. The Philips curve shows that low inflation usually accompanies high unemployment, and, conversely, high inflation is accompanied by low unemployment. The idea is that during times of low unemployment, people will ask for and get higher salaries, leading to inflation. In the New Economy, however, low unemployment and low inflation sometimes go hand in hand.

Planned Economies. When the government makes all the major decisions on how the economy is run. (See **Command Economies** and **Centrally Planned Economies**).

Poison Pill. When a company wants to defend itself against a hostile takeover, it may attempt to render itself unattractive through certain "unhealthy" financial maneuvers. A poison pill defense may involve a drastic increase in debt, or selling off valuable pieces of the company to ward off the evil takeover artists. Even if a poison pill defense succeeds in keeping the company in the hands of the original owners, however, it may end up irreparably harming the company it was meant to protect.

Preferred Stock. Stocks that pay a fixed dividend are called preferred stock. In many ways, a preferred stock is like a bond in that its fixed dividend resembles an interest payment. Preferred stock is considered senior to common stock—in the event of a bankruptcy, holders of preferred stock are paid before those holding common stock. Owners of preferred stock usually have no voting rights.

Primary Market. When new stocks and bonds are issued, they are often traded in a primary market until they are allowed to join the ranks of seasoned securities. A primary market for new bonds usually exists only until the payment date, when the life of the bond as an interest-paying security really begins. Primary market trading normally takes place outside established exchanges.

Prime Rate. The interest rate that U.S. banks charge their best corporate customers. The prime rate is often used as a guideline for determining other interest rates that a bank will charge on loans to riskier customers. Following the guideline of "low risk, low reward," a bank's prime corporate customers usually pay the lowest interest rates.

Principal. Anyone making a loan wants to get paid back—and earn a little interest along the way. The amount of a loan that has to be paid back to the lender is called its principal. A bond's principal is often referred to as its "face value."

Private Placement. A new issue of equity or debt securities that is too small to be treated as a full public placement—such as an IPO or a full-fledged bond issue—is referred to as a private placement. The securities issued in a private placement are often sold only to a small group of institutional investors. Usually, there are fewer reporting requirements on private placements, and the securities are usually not traded on the open market.

Privatization. A government's "going-out-of-business" sale, privatization involves the selling off of state-owned companies. Privatization is an easy way for governments to raise money and ease the drain of inefficient industries on state resources. Privatization reached its heyday in Britain under Margaret Thatcher, when the government put everything from mail service to electricity production in private hands.

Productivity. Output per hour. Productivity is defined as the amount of goods or services produced by a given unit of labor, capital, land, etc. One of the hallmarks of the New Economy has been a marked increase in productivity: new technology allows people to produce more in a given amount of time.

Profit. The proverbial carrot that counterbalances the stick of bankruptcy. A company's profit is what's left to give to the company's owners, the stockholders, after paying off all the bills. Profit is the driving force behind most economic activity in market economies. In accounting, a company's profit is also referred to as net income, or earnings.

Program Trading. Instead of buying an individual stock as an investment, program traders try to take advantage of discrepancies in markets, buying large amounts of stocks—or options or futures—in one market when prices are slightly out of line with prices in the others. They do this by programming computers to keep track of the prices of a basket of stocks, and then using that information to buy or sell large blocks of those stocks in markets around the world. Program trading has been blamed for a wide variety of market crashes, such as the Black Market crash in 1987 and the Asia Crisis in 1997.

Purchasing Power Parity (PPP). Unlike currency exchange rates, which are determined by the market, PPP looks at what money can actually buy in each country—calculating, in a sense, its purchasing "power." PPP looks at the price of a basket of goods and services—that includes everything from housing to haircuts, from food to movie tickets—which gives us a "real world" exchange rate.

Put Option. A put option gives the holder the right to sell something at a certain price. Like other options (see **Call Option**), a put can only be exercised for a certain length of time. An investor who thinks the price of an asset will go down will buy put options. As the underlying asset goes down in price, so does the put option.

Quota. In international trade, a quota is a limit on the quantity of a good that may be imported over a certain period. Contrary to tariffs, quotas are hard to get around—the price of the good can't be reduced to avoid them. Fortunately, quotas are usually the first barriers to go when countries sign free trade agreements.

Rational Expectations. Much of modern economic theory is based on the concept of rational expectations: that people, when armed with all available information, make rational decisions. Unfortunately, this is often not the case. Even when consumers and businesses know that a better-made product is being sold for a lower price, they sometimes opt for the one they "like." *Errare Humanum est*—to err is human, even in economics.

Real. Values that have been adjusted for inflation are referred to as "real." In inflationary times, it doesn't help to look at "nominal" salaries, it's important to adjust the figures for inflation. Real salaries tell us what people can actually do with the money they're earning.

Real Estate Investment Trust (REIT). Instead of buying property and holding onto it for years before selling it through a broker, the REIT investor buys a security, a piece of paper that represents ownership in a basket of real estate investments, such as shopping centers and apartment houses. The advantage of REITs, besides special tax benefits, is that the investor can buy and sell as they would a stock or a bond—on the open market.

Receivables. "Counting your chickens before they're hatched." On a balance sheet, something owed to the company is treated as an asset, even before it is paid. These assets are called "receivables." Once receivables are paid they become "current" assets.

Recession. A recession is a prolonged economic slowdown. Normally, a recession is declared after two successive quarters of negative economic growth. When a country is seen as entering a recession, interest rates are brought down to stimulate the moribund economy and reduce unemployment.

Repurchase Agreements, Repos. The purchase of securities, such as a bond, with the agreement to sell them back at a certain price and at a certain time in the future is essentially a form of short-term investment. Central banks, such as the U.S. Federal Reserve or the European Central Bank, often use repurchase agreements to inject money into—or remove it from—the economy. When traders hear that the Fed is doing "repos," they buy bonds as well, expecting a decline in interest rates.

Rescheduling. It is said that when a customer owes a bank a small amount of money and can't pay, the customer is in trouble, but when the customer owes the bank a *lot* of money and can't pay, the bank is in trouble. When confronted with problem borrowers who can't repay their loans, creditor banks sometimes reschedule the loans, essentially giving the debtors more time to come up with the money.

Road Pricing. In order to reduce pollution and overcrowding of roads, a system of electronic devices to monitor and charge for road usage has been set up in many cities in the world, from San Diego to London. By charging more for cars to use roads at certain times of the day, road pricing is a powerful economic incentive. It gets commuters to make more efficient use of roads or even switch to less expensive ways to get to work, such as carpools or public transportation.

Ruckus Society. A "non-violent guerilla action group." This Berkeley, California–based organization organizes protests, sometimes violently, against the forces of globalization in the world. It has targeted such organizations as the World Bank, the International Monetary Fund, and the World Trade Organization. Web site: www.ruckus.org.

Savings. In any economy, income that is not spent is called savings. A high savings rate means the economy has more money for businesses to invest because most savings are kept in banks where they can be lent out for other uses.

Savings and Loans (S&L). Savings and loans are financial institutions that use depositors' money to make loans, primarily to finance purchases of real estate such as homes and office buildings.

Securities and Exchange Commission (SEC). The SEC is a federal agency that oversees and regulates financial markets in the United States. The primary goal of the SEC is to protect the public from malpractice and fraud in the securities industry. The closest thing the world economy has to a SEC is the Bank for International Settlements based in Basel, Switzerland.

Security, Securitization. Worth more than the paper it's printed on. A security is a financial instrument that represents something of value. A security can be anything from a stock to a bond to a certificate of deposit. Even an IOU is a security because it is a promise to give to the holder something of value. Banks often securitize their assets—mortgages or credit card debt, for example—by grouping them in blocks and selling them as securities to other investors.

Short Sale. In most of the world's markets, investors are allowed to sell stock or other securities they do not own, as long as they agree to provide the securities at some time in the future. This practice is called short selling. Most short sellers borrow the shares from their brokers. Short sellers believe that a stock's price will go down and want to profit from this decline by selling early. They "cover" their short positions by buying the securities at a later date.

Sierra Club. One of the world's largest environmental group, the Sierra Club has taken a leading role in finding economic incentives, such as road pricing, to reduce pollution and environmental destruction throughout the world. Web site: www.sierraclub.org.

Smith, Adam. The father of modern economics. Adam Smith was an enlightened eighteenth-century Scotsman who believed that markets could take care of themselves. He introduced the world to such terms as the "invisible hand" of the marketplace and "division of labor." His book *The Wealth of Nations* provided the foundation for the modern capitalist economic system.

Socialism. The basic idea of socialism is that an economy should provide for an equitable distribution of wealth. There are many free-market socialist countries, where capitalism has been able to thrive within an egalitarian framework. Paris, for example, didn't stop being a thriving, elegant capital just because the French elected a socialist government.

Socially Conscious Investing. Socially conscious investors, such as college endowment funds, invest in equity funds that correspond to a specific view of how the world should be run. Some socially conscious equity funds invest only in companies that can show they are treating their foreign workers well or use sustainable resources, such as planting a tree for every one cut down.

Special Drawing Rights (SDR). A type of money created by the International Monetary Fund to provide an alternative to gold or other currencies. SDRs are used to keep accounts and make payments within the IMF framework. Many countries also use SDRs as a reserve currency. The value of an SDR is based on a basket of several major currencies, including the U.S. dollar, the Japanese yen, and the euro.

Speculation. A speculator buys or sells something for one reason: to profit from the investment's subsequent rise or fall in price. In contrast to hedgers and arbitragers, speculators think they know something the rest of the market hasn't yet figured out, and they act on it.

Spot Market. A trade executed for immediate delivery and payment is called a spot trade. The alternative to spot trading is buying or selling on the "forward" or "futures" market, where trades are executed at specific prices for delivery and payment sometime in the future.

Spread. The difference between the purchase price and the sale price. A currency exchanger, for example, will pay you less if you're selling a currency than if you're buying it. The difference in bid and offer prices, called spread, is a market-maker's secret to earning money. They make a profit by buying low and selling high, all day long.

Stagflation. Where economic stagnation meets inflation. "Stagflation" occurs in an economy with high inflation and low growth. This phenomenon rarely occurs, because inflation is usually the product of an overheated economy, not one that is stagnating. Stagflation is a worst-case scenario where inflationary pressures are so strong that even an economic downturn is unable to quell the pressure toward rising prices.

Standard & Poor's (S&P). One of the world's biggest ratings agencies, Standard & Poor's looks carefully through a company's books—or at a country's financial and economic situation—and makes a judgment about how creditworthy the company or country is. This judgment is given in terms of letters. AAA is used to describe the most creditworthy debtors. Web site: www.S&P.com.

Stock. Stock is ownership in a company. This ownership is represented by pieces of paper or electronic bookkeeping entries called shares. Stockholders—also called shareholders or shareowners—have a claim to the earnings and assets of a company.

Stock Index Future. A stock index future allows investors to benefit from the rise in a stock index, such as the Hang Seng Index in Hong Kong or the Standard & Poor's 500 in New York. Buying a stock index future is equivalent to buying all of the shares in the index. If the index goes up in value, the owner of the stock index future can profit handsomely.

Stock Option. Stock options give the holder the right to buy a certain number of shares, called underlying shares, at a certain price in the future. Many companies provide employees with stock options, allowing them to profit when the share's price goes up. The holder of a stock option, like any other option, has no risk in the sense that if the market declines, or doesn't rise enough, the stock option is just allowed to expire.

Stockholders' Equity. Sometimes referred to as net worth, stockholders' equity, or shareholders' equity, is a company's assets minus its liabilities. Basically, if a company were to use its assets, such as cash to pay off its debts, whatever would be left is referred to as stockholders' equity.

Structural Change. An economy undergoes "structural change" when factors of production such as labor markets and investment policy are radically altered. In the New Economy, technological advances and the use of the Internet allowed economies to grow and produce well beyond normal levels. Other forms of structural change involve taxes and labor markets.

Subsidy. Subsidies are government payments to businesses, ostensibly to help them through economic hard times. Most subsidies are criticized as a waste of taxpayer's money because they end up rewarding inefficiency: many badly managed and inefficient companies could not compete on the global markets without government subsidies.

Supply and Demand. A market economy works on the principle that the supply of any good is limited. The less there is of it— gasoline, for example—the more expensive it will be. A capitalist economy uses this phenomenon to let consumers and businesses decide how to allocate their resources.

Supply Side Economics. Supply side economics is based on the view that producers and consumers can stimulate economic growth better than governments. By providing companies and individuals with tax breaks, for example, a government reduces its revenue. But putting the extra money in the hands of efficient companies and consumers, it is assumed, provides new incentives for saving and investing, and stimulates the economy more efficiently than if the money were pumped into the economy through government spending.

Surplus. A surplus occurs whenever there is more coming in than going out. A trade surplus, for example, occurs when a country sells more abroad than it imports, which means a foreign exchange surplus. A government budget surplus occurs when tax receipts exceed expenditures.

Swap. At a swap meet, you can trade something you have for something you want, such as Barbie dolls or Pokemon cards. In the international financial markets, a swap is a trade agreement between two or more counter-parties, such as banks, to exchange different assets or liabilities. Essentially, a swap allows both parties to obtain the right assets or cash flows for their own particular needs. In the world economy, this most often means exchanging loans with different interest rates or different currencies.

Synergy. 1+1=3. Synergy occurs when two or more parties combine their particular skills or assets for mutual gain. In trade, synergy refers to the comparative advantage of letting each country produce and export those goods and services that it produces more efficiently than the others. In the end, the theory goes, when each country is allowed to do what it does best, everyone is better off.

Takeover. Anyone can take over a company, as long as they control enough shares. In a leveraged buyout, for example, takeover artists usually borrow large amounts of money to buy enough shares to acquire a company. They then restructure the company, usually selling off enough of the assets to pay the acquired debt and, hopefully, make a hefty profit.

Tangible Net Worth. Tangible net worth is an accounting tool that evaluates a company by looking only at its tangible assets and liabilities, which include everything from cars to cash to bank deposits and loans. This "real world" measure doesn't include assets such as goodwill and brand names, which have no quantifiable value. The tangible net worth of dot-com companies, for instance, is often negative. Without intangible assets, such as name recognition and market share, most New Economy companies would be worth nothing—their tangible assets usually consist of a bunch of computers and some potted plants.

Tariff. A tariff is a tax on imports. Tariffs are just one of many different trade barriers that a country can use to discourage imports. The advantage of tariffs is that they can be easily quantified and, therefore, easily removed.

Tax Haven. A country that offers extremely low taxes to individuals or companies is referred to as a tax haven. By reducing or eliminating taxes on profit or income, these countries— often small islands or enclaves—are able to attract lucrative trading business or high net-worth individuals such as tennis stars, rock singers, and, all too often, money launderes and illegal drug dealers.

Third Way. A new form of socialism. Developed by Tony Blair's Labour Party in Britain, the "Third Way" brought a free-market, pro-business aspect to the previously anti-growth party platform. It was modeled in part on Bill Clinton's remake of the Democratic Party in the United States. The Third Way plan was followed by many socialist governments around the world, including Gerhard Schröder's Democratic Socialist party in Germany.

Third World. The developing countries are often referred to as the Third World because at one time the world was divided into three areas: the First World of industrialized capitalist countries, the Second World of socialist countries, and the developing countries, also called "emerging economies."

Trade Balance. A country's trade balance sums up all of its international purchases and sales of goods and services, plus all international financial transfers such as interest payments on foreign debt. These figures tell us which countries are running a trade deficit and which ones are running a trade surplus. The trade balance is also referred to as the current account.

Sometimes, the merchandise trade balance (see **Merchandise Trade Balance**) is also referred to as a trade balance, even though it measures only "visible" goods that can actually be loaded onto a ship or plane.

Transparency International (TI). A Berlin-based organization, Transparency International fights graft and bribery in the world economy by working with international organizations such as the OECD to expose, investigate, and unmask corruption throughout the world. One of its most effective tools is publishing lists of countries and companies around the world that encourage and condone corrupt business practices. Web site: www.transparency.org.

UNCTAD. The United Nations Committee for Trade and Development (UNCTAD) is used to bring rich and poor countries together in periodic forums to work out specific problems related to international trade and development issues.

Underemployment. Economists define "underemployed" people as those working part-time or those working at a level that is significantly below their training or qualifications. Most unemployment rates don't usually include the underemployed—because they're not actively looking for a new job.

UNDP. The United Nations Development Program was set up to promote sustainable development around the world. Its goal is to help countries around the world create jobs, protect the environment, and, above all, eliminate poverty. Web site: www.undp.org.

Unemployment. Unemployment is one of the world's most important economic statistics. It tells politicians and economists how well an economy is working; when unemployment gets too low, the economy has to be slowed down. Some unemployment actually is considered good for an economy— there has to be a few people around looking for work to keep the economy running smoothly and to keep wages from skyrocketing.

Unilateral. Like one hand clapping in the dark. Unilateral trade barriers are imposed by one country, acting on its own to limit imports. These barriers are usually meant to temporarily protect local producers from foreign competition, giving them time to improve their productivity. The problem is that local producers, once given the comfort of a protected market, rarely make the sacrifices to improve their products or lower their prices. Unilateral trade barriers also often end up causing other countries to erect barriers of their own.

Value-Added Tax (VAT). A tax applied at each stage of production is called a value-added tax. Every time a product's value is increased, the person or company adding the value has to pay a tax. In contrast to a sales tax, which is paid at the moment of final sale, a value-added tax is paid by all parties in the production process. VAT is used in almost every modern industrial economy—except the United States. The idea of a VAT is to distribute the tax burden more evenly between producers and consumers.

Velocity. Economists use the word velocity to describe how quickly an economy grows in relation to the available money supply. The "speed" of money tells us what an economy can do with the money supply at its disposal. When a country produces a large Gross Domestic Product (GDP) with a small money supply, it is said to have "high velocity of circulation."

Venture Capital. *Nothing ventured, nothing gained.* Venture capital refers to money that is invested in a company that has not shown much profit, if any at all. The idea is to get in early. When the company finally shows a profit, venture capitalists reaps the rewards. Venture capital can be invested in anything from high-tech startups to gold-mining companies.

Volatility. The movement of a price over time is referred to as its volatility. A stock, for example, is said to be highly volatile if its price changes a lot and it changes often. Volatility measures both the frequency of movement as well as the magnitude of price changes. The volatility of stocks, bonds, commodities, and other investments is a major factor in determining their price. Most investors prefer to stay away from investments with highly volatile prices.

Wage-Price Spiral. The quintessential "vicious circle." A wage-price spiral involves rapid price rises followed by equally rapid demands for higher wages, which result in more price rises. Like the proverbial chicken-or-the-egg scenario, no one can really say which comes first, the rise in wages or the rise in prices.

Warrant. Just like in the Old West where a warrant gave a bounty hunter the right to seize someone for a fee, a warrant gives the holder a right, usually to buy a stock at a certain price over a certain period of time. Warrants are often attached to a bond in order to provide investors with a "kicker," enticing them to accept lower interest rates in exchange for the chance to benefit if the company's stocks rise.

Withholding Tax. A tax deducted at the time a dividend or other form of income is received is called a "withholding tax." In most countries, interest payments on bonds and stock dividends are subject to a withholding tax. This allows the tax authorities to receive their money before it goes into the pocket of the investor.

Workers Rights Consortium. A public-interest group active on college campuses throughout the United States. The Workers Rights Consortium's aim is to combat sweatshop conditions in Third World factories. Web site: www.workersrights.org.

World Trade Organization (WTO). The closest thing the world has to a trade watchdog is the World Trade Organization. Based in Geneva, Switzerland, the WTO is essentially a forum where disputing countries can meet to remove barriers to trade. If the WTO is asked to make a judgement, the "guilty" country is told to remove the illegal trade barrier. If it doesn't, the country that has suffered is allowed to erect trade barriers of its own, usually in the form of tariffs.

Yield. "Many happy returns." Yield, the return on an investment, is usually calculated in terms of percentage. When a bond is said to be yielding eight percent, the purchaser of the bond can count on receiving an average of eight percent per year until the bond is redeemed. Yields can be applied to almost any investment in the world economy, from real estate to bonds of Internet startups.

Zero Coupon Bond. A bond that pays no interest obviously has to have some kicker to attract investors. Zero coupon bonds are therefore sold at a discount. The buyer pays less than its face value, knowing that at some point in the future, the bond will be repaid in full.

Zero-Sum Game. A zero-sum game is based on the concept that one side's loss is exactly equal to the other side's gain. The concept was developed in the context of "game theory," where all economic and political decisions produce clear winners and losers, and nothing in between. In the real world, however, there are few zero-sum games. Inventing a better mousetrap doesn't hurt anyone except a few inefficient mousetrap makers—and, of course, the mice.